Library of
Davidson College

SHAKESPEARE
AS A DRAMATIST

SHAKESPEARE AS A DRAMATIST

BY
SIR JOHN SQUIRE

HASKELL HOUSE PUBLISHERS LTD.
Publishers of Scarce Scholarly Books
NEW YORK, N. Y. 10012
1971

First Published 1935

HASKELL HOUSE PUBLISHERS LTD.
Publishers of Scarce Scholarly Books
280 LAFAYETTE STREET
NEW YORK, N. Y. 10012

Library of Congress Catalog Card Number: 79-159971

Standard Book Number 8383-1221-7

Printed in the United States of America

TO
VISCOUNT AND VISCOUNTESS LEE
OF FAREHAM

CONTENTS

CHAPTER		PAGE
	PREFACE	ix

I. GENERAL CONSIDERATIONS: I . . . 1

Modern stage and production versus the Elizabethan stage. Would Shakespeare to-day write like Shaw? Modern playwrights and futility. The Elizabethan male audience and common humanity. Spirit of the modern age and the poets.

II. GENERAL CONSIDERATIONS: II . . 15

Shakespeare as dramatist neglected—the biographers—the editors—the syllable counters—the literary critics. Lamb, Hazlitt, Dr. Johnson, De Quincey, Coleridge, Swinburne, George Brandes.

III. GENERAL CONSIDERATIONS: III . . 33

What is dramatic technique? Author and audience. Craftsmanship and content. Mistakes a playwright must avoid. Changing conditions of the theatre. Subjects. Plot. Plays and novels. *Hamlet* as a novel. How two dramatists wrote *King John*.

IV. PLOT, CONSTRUCTION, DEVICE . . . 59

Shakespeare's imperfections. Given themes and made themes. History and the stage. Shakespeare's part in the historical plays. His handling of history. The ancient plays. Original stories versus dramatic plots: Cinthio, Boccaccio and Shakespeare. Loose threads. Rewritten plays. Modern theory and ancient practice. Shakespeare did the best things best. A number of flaws. Beginnings and initial expositions: starting of action and setting of tone. Suggesting a world beyond. The conduct of the fable. Characters, motivation, relation. Theatrical tricks. Allusions to the audience, suspense, background, times and seasons, contrast, mechanical stratagems, eavesdroppings. Endings and death.

CONTENTS

CHAPTER		PAGE

V. THE DRAMATIC PRESENTATION OF CHARACTER 138

    Means of presenting character. Novelist and dramatist. Shakespeare's power of characterization. Description of people off-stage; self-revelation through speech; self-revelation through action.

VI. DIALOGUE AS REVEALING CHARACTER AND FORWARDING ACTION 161

    Words as play-words. Shakespeare's sense of language. Words in character. The dramatist's necessary economy. Volubility and laconicism. Word, mood, action and person. Subtlety of construction, cadence and pace. Life in dialogue.

VII. DIALOGUE: MINOR DEVICES . . . 195

    "Writing down." The topical allusion. Amusing nonsense. Malapropisms. Catch-phrases. Ranting. Puns.

VIII. DIALOGUE: SOLILOQUIES AND LONG SPEECHES 206

    Modern theories about long speeches. Two classes of them: the dramatic and the interpolative. The test of soliloquies. Superb soliloquies. "Telling the audience." What modern managers would cut. "Getting away with it." The Muse of Fire. Dramatic poetry and the closet drama.

INDEX 227

PREFACE

THIS is the first part of a study of Shakespeare: the other two volumes projected, and now, for some years, begun, deal with Shakespeare as a poet, and with Shakespeare as a person, and chiefly in so far as he can be reasonably deduced from his plays.

There is no contribution to " historical research " in this book; play is not considered by play, nor will there be found here the usual sequence of " The Man," " The Editions," " The Tragedies," " The Comedies," " The Poems "; nor such treatment as is indicated by titles like " Youth," " Storm and Stress," and " Calm after Storm." Those who wish to learn about the design, and mechanics, of the Elizabethan playhouses may find all they want in the works of Sir Edmund Chambers and Mr. W. J. Lawrence, while Mr. Granville-Barker's invaluable *Prefaces* relate the mechanics to the plays. Those who wish to learn all, and more than all, that is known about the life of Shakespeare and the people whom he knew, or might have known, may be referred to the fruits of Sir Sidney Lee's devoted industry. Matters of origins, of Italian Novels and English Chronicles, of folios, good quartos, bad quartos, pirates, punctuation, and methods of production may be investigated in countless books by specialists—the latest of which, a little book called *Elizabethan Stage Conditions*, by Miss M. C. Bradbrook, came out just as this work was being concluded, and cheered the author by saying some things that he had already resolved to print himself. And a general encyclopædic conspectus of every part of the field, including my own, may be found in *A Companion to Shakespeare Studies*, edited by Mr. Granville-Barker and Mr. G. B. Harrison, which appeared more recently still.

I hope in my second volume to comment on some of the more controversial questions in these fields. All I have done at present—if I may substitute the personal pronoun for that awkward " the author " —is to read Shakespeare with as fresh an eye as possible. The determination arose from a discovery which is elaborated in the ensuing chapter: the discovery that even the poets and dramatists have discussed Shakespeare very little as a dramatist or a poet. If I have even partly proved my case in this volume, I shall be content; for in the next volume the case will be more easily provable still. Shakespeare's ' metrics,' in particular his ' feminine endings,' have been scrutinized as with watchmakers' glasses in the search for genuine passages in doubtful plays and doubtful passages in genuine plays; yet even the poets have written next to nothing about his characteristic melodies, his characteristic images, and those qualities of imagination in him which made him akin to the lunatic and the lover. Small blame to the critics: Shakespeare is a vast shoal of red herrings. But there seemed to me still to remain corners for the sympathetic

PREFACE

examination of an unacademic mind. Whatever faults this book may have are not due to lack of trouble.

I am deeply grateful to Mr. Harley Granville-Barker for reading my proofs and making many valuable suggestions. Now I read the proofs myself, I feel I must also apologize to him for quoting from him even more freely than I had thought.

I have used the Oxford Text, edited by Mr. W. J. Craig, and am indebted to Messrs. Macmillan and Company for permission to quote from *Queen Mary*, by Lord Tennyson.

J. C. S.

May 1935.

SHAKESPEARE AS A DRAMATIST

CHAPTER I

GENERAL CONSIDERATIONS: I

As a preliminary I must ask the reader never to lose sight of a few essential considerations; for though there are certain eternal canons of the dramatic art, things are possible and popular in one theatre and age which are not in another.

Even Lamb, even Bradley, reading men who saw more of Shakespeare's figments in their studies than they could see in their contemporary theatres, failed to realize that Shakespeare did not write for their theatres, but wrote for a stage with little but conventionalized scenery, wrote for an audience which could jump rapidly to scenic conclusions, wrote indeed for blind men remembering sight. Our modern stage is gradually being cleared of the clutter of battlements, lawns, weeping-willows and ships' decks which at once get between the author and his audience, and save the lazy author the trouble of conveying his whole fable through his words, though they hamper him, structurally, as Shakespeare and his contemporaries never were hampered. Scenery in itself is not necessarily bad. It can be extremely beautiful, as the contemporaries of Mr. Aubrey Hammond and Mr. Oliver Messel fully realize; and frequently it is compensation for a bad play, the ocular satisfaction making up for the aural disappointment. But where a play is intense, where a dramatist is endeavouring to concentrate our attention on the emotional and intellectual conflicts of his characters, elaborate scenery and properties compete, and the better they are the worse they are. The decay (or call it change) began in Shakespeare's own day: other men stuck masques into his plays. By the time of Dryden and Purcell (the *Faerie Queene* even contains a Chinese scene, consonant with the chinoiserie and tea which were just coming in, which would please the most modern producer of superior revue) spectacle had begun to kill the poets and corrupt the musicians; and the zenith (or nadir) was attained in our own day by Sir Herbert Tree, who had Macbeth's witches swinging round on wires amid volumes of flame-lit smoke, and a realistic nightingale-machine chirruping off-stage in *A Midsummer Night's Dream*. There was no nightingale off stage in Shakespeare's day. It was enough for Juliet to say:

> It was the nightingale, and not the lark,
> That pierc'd the fearful hollow of thine ear;
> Nightly she sings on yon pomegranate tree:
> Believe me, love, it was the nightingale,

and the audience, their imagination stimulated by the richest vocal inflections and pauses, could hear the doubtful song for itself as it came to Juliet's biased heart. The modern author, influenced by the theatre as he must be, fills half his 'script' with instructions about lighting, movement and the placing of chairs, subjecting his imagination on the lower plane to a strain which must impair its strength for operations on a higher plane. Shakespeare had little bother about chairs—he left this sort of thing to the actors, who also bothered very little about them: the producer's work, in any event, is better done on the stage than in the study. And during that brief glory—for the whole of our great drama was born and died within half a century, and then all things changed—there was no attempt to use mechanical stage-effects to the prejudice of what could be done by words and acting for an audience trained to use its imagination.

There is a passage very pertinent to this in Mr. Granville-Barker's preface to *King Lear*: it bears, incidentally, on the refusal of the beloved author of *Mr. II.* to admit that Lear was actable. I shall quote it rather fully:

Lear, Kent and the rest must *act* the storm then; there is no other way. They must not lose themselves in its description; it will not do for us to be interested in the storm at the expense of our interest in them, the loss there would be more than the gain. For the effect of the storm upon Lear is Shakespeare's true objective. So he has to give it magnitude without detracting for one precious moment during the crisis from Lear's own dramatic supremacy. And he solves his problem by making the actor impersonate Lear and the storm together, by identifying Lear's passion with the storm's. Mere association will not serve: there must be no chance left of a rivalry of interest. For that again might set the sensations of the audience at odds and dissipate the play's power upon them. This puts the thing crudely, and Shakespeare's skill in enriching and masking his main effect with minor ones (lest we grow too conscious of what he is doing and resist him) is amazing. But this is the basis of his stagecraft, to make Lear and the storm as one. And if Lamb saw " an old man tottering about the stage with a walking stick," he did not see the Lear of Shakespeare's intention:

> Blow, winds, and crack your cheeks! rage! blow!
> You cataracts and hurricanoes, spout
> Till you have drench'd our steeples, drown'd
>   the cocks!
> You sulphurous and thought-executing fires,
> Vaunt-couriers to oak-cleaving thunderbolts,
> Singe my white head! And thou, all-shaking
>   thunder,
> Strike flat the thick rotundity o' the world!
> Crack nature's moulds, all germens spill at once
> That make ingrateful man!

This is the storm itself in its tragic purpose, as Shakespeare's imagination gives it voice. And any actor who should try to speak the lines realistically in the character of a feeble old man would be a fool. There is no realism about it. No real man could or would talk so. But the convention enables Shakespeare to isolate Lear for the time from all pettier circumstance, to symbolize the storm in him, and so to make him the great figure which the greater issues of the play demand. The actor must make both himself and, for the moment, the lesser Lear—the Lear of infirmities and humours—forgotten as he speaks the lines; not such a hard thing to do if, without forgetting he is Lear, he yet speaks them for their own sake, for they outpace humanity. The lesser Lear will be recalled to us—and with interest—when Shakespeare wants him to be.

" There is no realism about it " . . . " they outpace humanity ": those sentences give the clue to another major difference between the modern and the Elizabethan dramas. In a word, theirs was a poetic drama, and ours is not.

The roots of the difference lie deep: a whole ' philosophy of history ' would have to be embarked upon, with countless inquiries into political, religious, social and economic circumstances, were any endeavour made to explain, however inadequately, why, in a few lonely ages, the stage has been dominated by great poets, and why in two thousand years and more so few plays (and those theirs) have lived. But the fact is there: the men, the materials, the methods, the objects, in the Elizabethan theatre differed from ours in connection with all those elements which make literature immortal. I saw recently a statement that if Shakespeare were alive to-day, he would be writing like Ibsen or Mr. Bernard Shaw. That statement, though it does show an apprehension of the profound change in the theatre, is, literally, I think, not even a half-truth. It is no more true than it would be to say that Mr. Ibsen and (still less) Mr. Shaw would have been among the glories of the Elizabethan theatre. The Ibsen of *Brand* and *Peer Gynt* was on the razor-edge between wandering plays about eternal problems and tight analytical plays about feminism and drains. He might, however, had he been born English, have ranked among the minor Elizabethan dramatists; he would have managed verse of a kind and contrived a good, if rather acid, topical appeal. Anyhow, the situation is clearer and simpler if we confine ourselves to citizens of our own country. Mr. Shaw as an Elizabethan dramatist is inconceivable: imagine him at the Mermaid calling for water and the whites of poached eggs, while the rest indulged in poetry which he considered cheap romance, and humour which he considered cheap and bibulous buffoonery. Imagine him trying to persuade Burbage to produce, or the audience to listen to, a play aimed at improving the sanitation of London, though it definitely needed improvement. Shakespeare suited his age; Mr. Shaw suits his: they could never have been interchangeable, and neither could have flourished in the theatre of the other one's age. Mr. Shaw has produced his own notion of Shakespeare in *The Dark Lady of the Sonnets*: a light vivacious ass, only a little better than Mr. Shaw's Dubedat. Mr. Shaw seems to draw his ideas about artists of all kinds from second-rate café-haunters. Genius as he is, he does not understand the beginnings of poetry, the violence of a poet's emotions, his struggles to make terms between this world and the next, his endeavours to reconcile dream, science and common sense, his faculty for assuaging torment by music. Mr. Shaw is supremely witty, very fluent, has a vast natural vocabulary, and can see through many obvious shams. But he sometimes knocks his head against things that are not shams. His Shakespeare bears no more relation to a real great poet (such as Hardy, Bridges and Housman have been, in our own time, in England) than his imbecile medicine-men in *The Doctors' Dilemma* bear to the great servants of humanity one has known. His Shakespeare bears about the same relation to the real Shakespeare as a quack with a bedside manner bears to Lord Lister.

So many ages, so many men. The minor dramatists of Shakespeare's era may not have been much cleverer men than the minor dramatists of our own era: Massinger may not have been much cleverer than Maugham, or Marston than Galsworthy. But they were a different kind of man: the poets, the men who love passion and verbal music and the general human tragedy and comedy, without too much thinking of the stage as a place for reforming zeal or disappointed cynicism, were in the theatre, acting, producing, with an audience (mainly male) aristocratically financed, with an illiterate but emotional and musically-responsive proletariat, or ' general,' yelling in the background. Since Dryden, the poets have not really been in the theatre at all: economic, political and social changes have driven them out and let in the reformers, the realists, the smart topical wits, who would never have had a chance in Elizabethan England or Athens. The Athenian and Elizabethan dramatists were topical enough in a casual and subordinate way; but it is possible to enjoy them, whether Aristophanes (who was very topical) or Shakespeare, skipping the things that notes are needed for, and concentrating on eternal music, wonder, humour and truth. Our own drama, whether it be propagandist or topically satirical, is a branch of journalism. The gods, life and death are forgotten: all the concentration is on possible Acts of Parliament suggested by persons who have made no attempt to study the past, no attempt to face the world with all its differences of races and climates, no attempt to consider all the hypotheses which the soul of man has formulated to explain the mystery of existence, of responsibility towards the Deity, of the difference between Good and Evil, of the relations between Universal Good and fleeting morals, or of the meaning of the first chapters of Genesis as they bear on the relations between God, Man and Woman.

He for God only, she for God in him.

That was Milton about Adam and Eve: he at least had a simple theory. No such theory can be perceived in most of our modern solemn problem-plays. They are either Rousseauistically idealistic, refusing facts, or cynically realistic, refusing other facts. As for marriage, they appear to know that Mr. Shaw and Mr. Bertrand Russell have written about it, but do not seem to have heard of Westermarck, or to have even glimpsed the fact that all history is a crucible in this regard as in others or that discovery by trial and error has been proceeding ever since the Stone Age, and at this moment is still proceeding in all the simultaneous ' ages ' of the world, from Stone to Poison Gas. The dramatists (and the novelists) frankly reflect the preoccupations of the intelligent, half-educated women who are the main support of the contemporary drama and the contemporary novel. They want to refuse facts; they are indignant that men should have been made different from women; they think they are in ' a Doll's House '; they are determined to be let out—whither?

Nowhere, probably. The Fall is symbolical, and the Creation symbolical. The story of the Garden of Eden is equally discreditable to both parties. If only both parties would realize that, and would realize that they were only in this world for a certain space of time, things would, for both parties, be much easier. The trouble is that the faith in the other world has gone. " Darling, do stay with me. I can do so much if you back me up, and urge me on to all my causes "—that is what the man says. " Darling, you must realize that I want to do things on my own, and see things for myself, and think for myself (even if I'm wrong), and I do think that Mr. Shaw and Mr. Bertrand Russell have opened new paths, and I do think that Mr. Coward is exposing the horrors of contemporary society."

Thus do they talk after the modern plays. They could not have talked thus after the first nights of Shakespeare. He was helped, of course. In the first place, he had a mainly male audience. In the second place, he had boys acting as women; and the combination of actors and audience helped him to avoid concentrating on 'domestic dramas,' 'eternal triangles' and, to the exclusion of all else, on the relations of men and women to each other as men and women, and not simply as people. Go through the plays of Shakespeare and you will find that there are not only very few love-intrigues, but even very few kisses, weepings, and baby-nursings. The boy-actors kept him off all these things to some extent: the point is obvious, and need not be elaborated. But his own nature and propensity kept him off still more. Thinking of men and women more in terms of our common hankering humanity than in terms of a God-forgetting, past-forgetting, family-forgetting, self-fulfilling desire to obtain things from life that cannot be obtained, and take things from life without giving more than the equivalent, he concentrated on things which concern us all, men and women, more than do our fleeting relations with each other. "To be, or not to be?" was Hamlet's question: not "to divorce or not to divorce?"

" Shakespeare would have written like Ibsen and

Mr. Shaw "; what rubbish! There have been poets since Shakespeare. The last who half-conquered the theatre—and then only by compromising between the eloquence of the heart and the witty smut that the age demanded—was Dryden. Since then there have been many great poets in England. Almost all of them have attempted to write plays. But the divorce between the spirit of the age (especially as manifested in the ownership and control of the stage) has been such that not one of them has succeeded. Had poetry died, one might have blamed the poets. But with Wordsworth, Coleridge, Byron, Shelley, Keats, Tennyson, Matthew Arnold, Browning, Bridges, and Hardy all producing great poetry, most of them attempting plays, all of them failing in the theatre, must one not blame the age rather than the poets? Who cannot but suppose that in the Elizabethan era Thomas Hardy would have been immeasurably greater than Mr. Coward or Mr. Lonsdale? Who that ever saw the reduced edition of his *Dynasts* at the Kingsway can have failed to observe that it was immeasurably better than anything that the late Sir Arthur Pinero ever wrote? *The Magistrate* might very well, had Sir Arthur been born in that time, have competed, as farce, with *Bartholomew Fair* or *The Shoemaker's Holiday*. But *Mid-Channel* and *The Second Mrs. Tanqueray* are inconceivable in an Elizabethan setting. Shakespeare would have laughed heartily (having created Shallow) at the first; he would have been simply bored by the other two. The truth is that the poets are not to-day in the theatre. They exist, struggling; and a few will read them. But they are not wanted in the theatre; and, were Shakespeare alive to-day, and himself, he would be told that Mr. Noel Coward could do what was wanted very much better.

All this is said with a view to the following pages. The age does not like Shakespeare: he can only just go down in the West End if an actor like Mr. John Gielgud does a magnificent performance of some part, and people come to see the acting. It simply must be borne in mind that this concentration on the eternities, this delight in musical speech, this acceptance of interrupting songs and soliloquies were natural to our ancestors. Were they only natural to us! I have seen plays by Galsworthy in which breakfast-tables, offices and auction-rooms were faithfully reproduced. I have seen a play (which ended with a beautiful, and truly Elizabethan, scene) by Mr. Maugham, which contained a perfect reproduction of a barber's shop. I have seen strikers' meetings, and suffragettes' meetings, with scenery. Not a single appurtenance was wrong! The Regency auctioneers' desks in Devizes, the Lions in Trafalgar Square; these, and a hundred other things, were faithfully reproduced. Shakespeare knew nothing of all that, and Thomas Hardy, until late in life, wrote nothing for the theatre. At eighty or so he adapted *Tess*; when he was seventy or so *The Dynasts* was reduced for the theatre. In the Elizabethan age he would have (barring Shakespeare) dominated the stage. He understood the tragic exaggeration of character also; our age will allow photography or the exaggeration in the direction of satirical caricature, but hardly the exaggeration (though it be as revealing as caricature) of poetic grandeur. Coleridge observed what the Elizabethans did in this direction:

In the plays of Shakespeare every man sees himself, without knowing that he does so: as in some of the phenomena of Nature, in the mist of the mountain, the traveller beholds his own figure, but the glory round the head distinguishes it from a mere vulgar copy. In traversing the Brocken, in the north of Germany. at sunrise, the brilliant beams are shot askance and you see before you a being of gigantic proportions, and of such elevated dignity, that you only know it to be yourself by similarity of action. In the same way, near Messina, natural forms, as determined distances, are represented on an invisible mist, not as they really exist, but dressed in all the prismatic colours of the imagination. So in Shakespeare: every form is true, everything has reality for its foundations; we can all recognize the truth, but we see it decorated with such hues of beauty, and magnified to such proportions of grandeur, that, while we know the figure, we know also how much it has been refined and exalted by the poet.

The same thought was concisely put by Francis Burrows in his sonnet on *Antony and Cleopatra*:

Titanic agony of what giants wasting
Near death, on what a mountainous eminence.

It might have been written of people in Æschylus and Sophocles; but hardly of people in modern plays. They may waste, but they are not giants. To-day, for poets, there is no outlet. The finest play by a modern poet was Flecker's *Hassan*; it was significant that the greatest scene was the one worst performed. The tide may turn.

CHAPTER II

GENERAL CONSIDERATIONS : II [1]

I

THE art of writing for the stage is a special art, with canons of its own, and achievements, limitations and perils peculiar to itself. To the practice of that art Shakespeare consecrated the whole of his active life. And, although he did not reach perfection at a bound and was always a careless artist, it is universally acknowledged that no man who ever lived

[1] So far as possible in this book, I have, when making quotations or giving instances, confined myself to those plays or parts of plays which I believe to have been written by Shakespeare. It would be ridiculous (though it is commonly done) to condemn him for a technical mistake on account of a passage of which the sentiment, language and rhythm make one think it impossible that he could have written it. This applies not merely to those plays—such as *Pericles*, *Titus*, and *Henry VIII*, which even the most coprophagous of Folio-worshippers admit to be of joint authorship—but also to parts of other plays. In *Romeo and Juliet*, for instance, there are passages which Shakespeare, however young, and however much 'under the influence' of 'mighty Marlowe' (who might have influenced him) or 'sportive Kyd' (who could not have influenced him, even as a business man), could no more have written than Burns could have written *The Ring and the Book* or Wordsworth *The Reel of Tullochgorum*. For a thorough investigation of this problem I commend the reader (though he must take half a grain of salt with him) to the volumes of Mr. J. M. Robertson's *The Shakespeare Canon*, which (however much too far Mr. Robertson may go in his nice distribution of responsibilities among Greene, Peele, Kyd, Marlowe and others, all of whom his good-tempered Shakespeare had to lick into shape) will certainly open the eyes of any candid reader who has taken for granted the attributions of scholars, whose susceptibility to tradition is often stronger than their sense of style.

was so lavishly endowed with the particular gifts which the dramatic art requires or could exercise them so easily; that none has displayed so sure an intellectual grasp of the exigencies of the stage, or has endowed the world with so rich and varied a series of dramatic triumphs. It was to the service of the Drama that he brought all the manifold powers of his genius, all his vast wisdom, all his passion, all the wealth of his poetic endowment. It will be urged presently that even his qualities as a poet have been unduly neglected. But the qualities of Shakespeare the Dramatist have been still more generally overlooked. That there are books, of sorts, on Shakespeare's technique may be granted. There is Professor Baker's valuable little book, and there is the work of Professor Brander Matthews; there is also Mr. R. G. Moulton's cold, efficient, limited and even perverse study. Others doubtless exist. There are books on every conceivable aspect of Shakespeare. There is a book arguing that he was a Roman Catholic, there is a book arguing that he was an Atheist, there is a book arguing that he was a Jew, and there are a thousand books arguing that he was Bacon or some other eminent peer. There are many books about Shakespeare's Heroines, and there is even a book about Shakespeare's Insects. Yet if the 'classical' and 'standard' criticism of Shakespeare from the earliest times down to our own be considered calmly, it must be discovered, however surprising the discovery may be, that there is very little of it which is concerned with Shakespeare's powers and methods as a writer for the stage, very little indeed that shows any awareness that there is a special technique of the stage which was a lifelong fascination to Shakespeare, to the development of which he enormously contributed, and within the limits of which he performed miracles.

A great part of Shakespearean literature is concerned with special aspects of his knowledge, with his ' sources,' with the textual history of his plays, with his relations to his time—in other words with facts, real or presumed. Much of this is useful, interesting, even diverting; the work of scholars who labour for our profit within limitations set by themselves. The late Sir Sidney Lee, whose *Life of Shakespeare* is the standard compilation of facts and hypotheses about the history of the dramatist and his works, was the archetype of the class. He specifically abnegated what he oddly termed " merely æsthetic criticism "; yet much that he did will be of great service to ' mere ' æsthetic critics. Such writers have their own work to do. So also have Shakespeare's editors. So also have those investigators (though these, as we shall see, might be assisted by more attention to dramatic technique) who, scouring the Elizabethan library for parallel passages, counting syllables, ' stopped lines ' and weak endings, comparing quartos, and arguing about phrases, attempt to decide the exact order of the plays and the authorship of various passages in those which are of joint authorship or doubtful attribution. These last are of primary importance. If anything approaching agreement be ever reached as to precisely what Shakespeare did and did not write or revise, it will be very much easier to diagnose his precise qualities and proclivities. These scholars, great and small, we must for the time put aside. It is only with ' literary ' critics, the eminent, the penetrating and the sensitive, who have devoted themselves to the study of Shakespeare's mind and creation and expression, that we are concerned here. An examination of their writings will confirm the statement that the nature of his dramatic endeavours and achievements has been, to a large extent, ignored by them; that they have been so engaged by wonder at the man and at the world of imaginary people that he created, so detained by the desire to expound his opinions and investigate the psychological problems which he put before us, so moved to glorify the grandeur of his intellect, the range of his sympathy, the variety of the life that sprang from his brain, that they have gone no farther. This is true of them from Dryden onwards.

It is frequently stated that two of the three finest Shakespearean critics who have written were Charles Lamb and Hazlitt. Certainly none have written more nobly of Shakespeare himself or with more penetration of his characters, and the Shakespearean pages of each contain some of the most bewitching prose in English. Yet, in spite of their belief that Shakespeare was not in the least concerned with getting his plays printed, each was ready to maintain that some or all of them were meant for reading, not for the stage; or, at least, that if they were not so meant, Shakespeare did not know what he was about.

Lamb went the farther. "I cannot help," he said, "being of opinion that the plays of Shakespeare are less calculated for performance on a stage, than those of almost any other dramatist whatsoever." He rejoiced, he said, in those plays of Shakespeare "which have escaped being performed." He complained that the supernatural in the theatre meant nothing to him. "Is *The Tempest* of Shakespeare at all a subject for stage representation?" he asked. *King Lear* (it must be remembered that Lamb knew only the modern spectacular theatre, not Shakespeare's, in which everything depended on gesture and speech) could not be represented on the stage. As for *Macbeth*, "the reading of a tragedy is a fine abstraction. It presents to the fancy just so much of external appearances as to make us feel that we are among flesh and blood, while by far the greater and better part of our imagination is employed upon the thoughts and internal machinery of the character." As an instance of what he meant he mentioned the concreteness of Macbeth's coronation robe on the stage: "But in reading, what robe are we conscious of? Some dim images of royalty—a crown and sceptre—may float before our eyes, but who shall describe the fashion of it?" We may allow a discount for the celebrated whimsicality; but the man who wrote this could scarcely be expected to devote much attention to dramatic principles and the nature of theatrical effects. Nor could he be expected himself to be successful in the theatre: the strange thing is that he attempted it. Lamb loved the imaginary worlds that the dramatist gave him, and he loved his memories of the old actors; but essentially he thought of an actor in Shakespeare as a man who reduced the beautifully impalpable to the all-too-solid, and he was more aware of the necessary limitations of the dramatic art than of the splendours that it alone can achieve.

As Miss Bradbrook says of the nineteenth-century successors of Lamb:

The numerous books on his *Mind and Art* or his *Dramatic Art* considered him solely as a delineator of character, or related his plays to a central moral precept. Dowden compared him at length with Bacon, Hooker, Raphael and Michael Angelo, but in the first twenty-five pages of his book there are only three quotations from the text. So far was Shakespeare separated from the stage that much of the inferior criticism was only a kind of mental performance of each play by the critic, at which the reader attended. Emotion was underlined, appearances and behaviour of various characters described, and their inner sensations suggested exactly as any competent actor might do. " Juliet turns her pale face appealingly to her father " (Dowden) replaced " We must assume that at this point Juliet grows pale." It was doubtless a satisfactory arrangement which allowed middle-aged gentlemen to play Mercutio if they wished, or to roar lustily as Othello.

Hazlitt was in another category. He was a lover of the theatre, and, on occasion, an acute dramatic critic. He said that "*The Midsummer-Night's Dream*, when acted, is converted from a delightful fiction into a dull pantomime." He even went farther (perhaps farther than he meant) with the sweeping statement: "Poetry and the stage do not agree." Shakespeare presumably differed from him here, though it must be admitted that there is more loss to set against the gain when the fairy plays go from study to stage (at least in our time) than when we witness the general run of Shakespeare's dramas in the theatre. Hazlitt's instinct for the theatre is evident frequently; yet his preoccupation was with the play of passion, the depths and complexities of character, the mind and genius of Shakespeare, rather than with the mode in which these were exhibited in the theatre as distinguished from other fields of artistic expression.

This is no ground for complaint against Hazlitt. Further—though it seems hardly necessary to state it—it would be grotesque to suggest that the aspects of Shakespeare with which he concerned himself are not the most momentous aspects. Technique is only a means to an end, and the theatre is less important than truth. An admirably constructed play might be written (and often is) by a person of second-rate intelligence, commonplace locution and low morality: indeed, in the modern theatre, mastery of technique often seems to exist in inverse proportion to intelligence and morality. All that is being suggested here is that the preoccupation of critics with those sides of Shakespeare, the man and the creator, which would have provoked precisely the same comment had he chosen to express himself in the novel, has been disproportionate; that, both for its own sake and for the light which it would have thrown upon numerous problems, we are the poorer for lack of a more systematic study of Shakespeare's art by critics of the greatest penetration and the swiftest perception. From the horde of famous Germans, those of them who are not burrowing in the scholastic dust, we get vast philosophical speculations and elaborate analyses of character: colonies of Germans have settled in the soul of Hamlet. The great English critics give us but scattered observations which are strictly dramatic criticism.

Many such observations are to be found in Dr. Johnson—in the last resort, perhaps the soundest of them all where matters of structure and truth to character are concerned, the others being mostly romantic rhapsodists over fine things. Johnson commented on Shakespeare's occasional lazy manner of finishing his plays; he remarked his fondness for interrupting his action by quibbles: "A quibble is to Shakespeare what luminous vapours are to the traveller. . . . A quibble is the golden apple for which he will always turn aside from his career, or stoop from his elevation." The author of *Irene* discussed and defended Shakespeare's defiance of the unities; he argued that not one of Shakespeare's plays was perfect or " wrought to his own ideas of perfection "; he stated that Shakespeare was content, with plot and dialogue, to make shift with anything that would ' go down '; and in a passage of some acuteness he noticed Shakespeare's tendency (not unnatural in a great poet) to interrupt his movement with long speeches, and his habit of endeavouring to carry these off by loading every rift with gold:

In narration he affects a disproportionate pomp of diction and a wearisome train of circumlocution, and tells the incident imperfectly in many words, which might have been more plainly delivered in few. Narration in dramatic poetry is naturally tedious, as it is unanimated and inactive, and obstructs the progress of the action; it should therefore always be rapid, and enlivened by frequent interruption. Shakespeare found it an encumbrance, and instead of lightening it by brevity, endeavoured to recommend it by dignity and splendour.

De Quincey—alas that he was not more systematic!—was more engaged than any of these with the dramatic aspect of the drama. Admiration for Shakespeare certainly carried him beyond " this side idolatry." Such a passage as this, which concludes his famous and masterly description and examination of " The Knocking at the Gate in

Macbeth," is like one of the gorgeous ravings of the Opium-Eater:

O mighty poet! Thy works are not as those of other men, simply and merely great works of art; but are also like the phenomena of nature, like the sun and the sea, the stars and the flowers; like frost and snow, rain and dew, hailstorm and thunder, which are to be studied with entire submissions of our own faculties, and in the perfect faith that in them there can be no too much or too little, nothing useless or inert—but that, the farther we press in our discoveries, the more we shall see proofs of design and self-supporting arrangement where the careless eye had seen nothing but accident.

This is the highest peak in the Alps of unqualified panegyric that the romantic generation raised; yet it comes at the close of a superb piece of dramatic criticism. Magnificently he places his scene, the two guilty beings, in the great suspense and hush after they have done the awful deed that has cut them off " by an immeasurable gulf from the ordinary tide and succession of human affairs," and superbly he reaches his climax:

We must be made sensible that the world of ordinary life is suddenly arrested—laid asleep—tranced—racked into a dread armistice; time must be annihilated; relation to things without abolished; and all must pass self-withdrawn into a deep syncope and suspension of earthly passion. Hence it is, that when the deed is done, when the work of darkness is perfect, then the world of darkness passes away like a pageantry in the clouds: the knocking at the gate is heard: and it makes known audibly that the reaction has commenced; the human has made its reflux upon the fiendish; the pulses of life are beginning to beat again; and the re-establishment of the goings-on of the world in which we live, first makes us profoundly sensible of the awful parenthesis that had suspended them.

It is in the theatre that de Quincey hears that knocking; would not Charles Lamb admit that the difference there between study and theatre was infinitely more than compensation for the reduction to mere gold and ermine of his dim regalia? De Quincey shows an equal sense of the stage in his acute and comprehensive summary of the characteristic qualities of Shakespeare's dialogue:

Now, in Shakespeare, who first set an example of that most important innovation, in all his impassioned dialogues, each reply or rejoinder seems the mere rebound of the previous speech. Every form of natural interruption, breaking through the restraints of ceremony under the impulses of tempestuous passion; every form of hasty interrogative, ardent reiteration when a question has been evaded; every form of scornful repetition of the hostile words; every impatient continuation of the hostile statement; in short all modes and formulæ by which anger, hurry, fretfulness, scorn, impatience, or excitement under any movement whatever, can disturb or modify or dislocate the formal bookish style of commencement—these are as rife in Shakespeare's dialogue as in life itself; and how much vivacity, how profound a verisimilitude, they add to the scenic effect as an imitation of human passion and real life, we need not say.

Pertinent observations, too, to the number of a dozen or so, may be found in the marvellous miscellany of Coleridge's Shakespearean criticisms, that assembly of golden fragments collected from newspaper reports, from shorthand notes of his rambling but inspired lectures, from his conversations at table. Some of his dicta as to Shakespeare's dramatic practice, delivered in rhapsodies of abject adoration, are untrue. Not a word, said he, was *ever* thrown by Shakespeare as a sop to the mob. (He did not wait for anyone to remind him of Lancelot Gobbo.) " Shakespeare never consciously wrote what was below himself." If he be upheld here, and in his equally sweeping statement that " the unity of feeling, is everywhere and at all times observed by Shakespeare in his plays " (which include *Measure for Measure* and which were then thought to include all of *Henry VIII*); if he even be supported in his statement that the dramatist 'never' followed his borrowed story when it hampered him—though Coleridge himself excused the improbability of the pound of flesh in *The Merchant of Venice* on the ground that " it was an old tale "— at least he is demonstrably speaking with insufficient reservation (assuming the reports of his speech to be accurate) when he says: " The characters of the dramatis personæ, like those in real life, are to be inferred by the reader;—they are not told to him."

Nobody ever described characters 'off-stage' in a more masterly way than Shakespeare, or more habitually: what in others is almost always a fault was in him almost always an added merit—as will presently be illustrated. But Coleridge was perhaps the first adequately to expound the unique merit, and the nature, of Shakespeare's opening scenes, " with the single exception of *Cymbeline* "— an exception that must always be made—and he was especially happy on the incomparable opening of *Romeo and Juliet*, though the droning Coleridge of Carlyle's description is evident in the phrase about the servants " who are under the necessity of letting the superfluity of Sensorial power fly off through the escape-valve of wit-combats." He notices in *Macbeth* " the novelty given to the most familiar images by a new state of feeling "; and refers to the porter's monologue in the same play as ' disgusting '—the inadequacy of the words to the situation being, of course, what he meant. Points that he seized were Shakespeare's skill in easy ' exposition ' and his great use of small things:

Schiller has the material sublime to produce an effect, he sets you a whole town on fire, and then throws infants with their mothers into the flames, or locks up a father in an old tower. But Shakespeare drops a handkerchief, and the same or greater effects follow.

In our own day another great poet, who was also a respectable playwright, said much less than he must have known as to Shakespeare's dramatic gifts. In point of fact, Swinburne, in his *Study of Shakespeare*, says very little, though he says that with prodigious eloquence. The book is a Carnival of Flowers, all beautiful exordiums and perorations and promises unfulfilled. With what an expectation, knowing his contempt for the finger-counting critics, we pass from his quiet opening which seems surely to prelude an ordered flood of new light. " The aim," he says, " of the present study

is simply to set down what the writer believes to be certain demonstrable truths as to the progress and development of style, the outer and the inner changes of manner as of matter, of method as of design, which may be discerned in the work of Shakespeare."

He is especially vehement as to a poet's claim to distinguish Shakespeare's voice by ear. Disappointment follows. He divides Shakespeare's work into periods and says that if the dates do not fit, so much the worse for the dates; he makes a great deal of the gradual abandonment of rhyme; he has a certain amount to say, based entirely on assertions (often convincing but unaccompanied by analysis) as to characteristics of thought and speech about the authorship of the mixed and the apocryphal plays. For the rest he presently sails away into ' tributes ' to Shakespeare and glowing descriptions of **Iago** and Falstaff, whom he calls "dear and honourable Sir John"; in the end being so carried away from all sense of music and of structure as to attribute to Shakespeare almost the whole of *Pericles*, including (very likely) the grotesque prologues spoken by Gower. His remarks on character are acute; his promise of an ear-test is supported by not a line of indication as to the marks of Shakespeare's vocabulary, imagery and melody. As to "method and design," he drops occasional hints which show that he too might have given us more illumination had he been less preoccupied with the glory of Imogen's "immortal godhead of womanhood" and the length of the late Dr. Furnivall's ass's ears. Swinburne observed the structural weaknesses of *Henry VIII* and *King John*; he remarked the weakness of the subordinate characters in *Richard II*; he noted, as perhaps none had noted before, the casual manner in which Shakespeare completely forgets Cordelia's loving husband at the end of *Lear*. The forced betrothal of Oliver to Celia in *As You Like It* he terms an ugly "little smear in one corner of the canvas"; and he violently objects to the grossly inartistic way in which a tragic end is avoided in *Measure for Measure*, and we the audience, who have been hungering for at least a grain of righteous retribution, are "tricked out of our dole, defeated of our due, lured and led on to look for some equitable and satisfying upshot, defrauded and derided and sent empty away." He was speaking as a dramatic critic when he described Shakespeare's ever-increasing mastery over characterization, and the way in which his later dramatic style " found its infinite gain in the loss of those sweet superfluous graces which encumbered the march and enchained the attendance of its childhood." It is less certain, though he skirted the truth, that he was not merely thinking of Shakespeare's Thersites' vein when he described *Troilus and Cressida* as a " magnificent monster of a play." In any event, he could not stop to demonstrate with examples, but must away to his breathless humanistic pæans, rejoicing in the roll of his exuberant tropes.

As a final specimen we may take Dr. George Brandes,[1] the most striking features of whose enormous and internationally applauded book will be indicated elsewhere. Here is a polymorphic book full of hypotheses about Shakespeare, an encyclopædia (if unwontedly coloured for such) of the Elizabethan scene, containing chapters on every play illustrated by what, were they drawn from any other poet, would be a plethora of quotations. Dr. Brandes observes such things as the varied visible pageantry of *Hamlet*; in an occasional dictum he goes so far as to touch on dramatic theory. He even remarks that surprise without preparation loses most of its force. Yet he leaves it at that, a truth which might have been so beautifully driven home by instances from Shakespeare's practice; and in a general way, all-embracing as he sets out to be,

[1] The references to Dr. Brandes were written before that celebrated man died. I have not altered them.

he neglects every aspect of dramatic technique with unexampled thoroughness. Chapter headings such as those concerning *Julius Cæsar*—" Fundamental Defects " and " Merits of the Play "—might at least be supposed to cover dramatic ground; but no—the burden of Dr. Brandes' theme is Shakespeare's ignorance of Rome, his intentions as to Brutus, and above all the libellous nature of his portrait of Cæsar as compared with the real Cæsar, or at any rate Mommsen's Cæsar—to whom he devotes several pages of almost servile biography.

A special treatise on this subject may therefore be permitted: a review on Shakespeare's mastery of every branch of the *dramatic* art, and on his lapses. By his lapses I do not mean his attribution of a sea-coast to Bohemia. Why, incidentally, this harmless, and perhaps conscious error, which even, to my mind, assists his production of a remote and færial atmosphere, should be so frequently grinned at is beyond me. Shakespeare committed other anachronisms and anatopisms than that. In *The Merchant of Venice* Gratiano hankers after ten godfathers more for Shylock " to bring thee to the gallows "—an allusion to the English jury system. In *Cymbeline* he mixes ancient Roman and modern Italian names; in *Antony and Cleopatra* he refers to the biblical Bulls of Bashan; in *Two Gentlemen of Verona* Robin Hood is familiarly mentioned in Italy; in *Troilus and Cressida* a Trojan talks Latin, Aristotle is referred to, and Pandarus (though this is in a semi-epilogue) talks of a " goose of Winchester "; in *Titus*

Andronicus Aaron speaks of " popish tricks and ceremonies "; and in *The Winter's Tale* we are introduced to Apollo (as a reigning god) and the Emperor of Russia. This sort of 'error' resembles a good many other things in the theatre: everything depends on whether the audience 'minds,' whether its illusion is, however slightly, impaired. Major and minor considerations, we may now pass a number of them under review. I cannot hope that many of my observations are new, except perhaps those with which nobody will agree; but there may be something of novelty in their grouping, and in the position that, as a body, they occupy in this small book.

CHAPTER III

GENERAL CONSIDERATIONS: III

WHAT do we mean by the technique of the dramatic art, the principles of constructing a work intended for theatrical representation? We mean the whole method by which a dramatist presents his fable to the audience: all the means by which he endeavours to convey a certain progress of events, a certain intellectual and emotional content, to a number of people who sit in a theatre and watch and listen to actors on a stage. We mean all the manipulations of words, persons and scenes, which aim, or should aim, at carrying the theme across the footlights in the most effective way: the means taken to secure the most effective order and proportion, the exactest communication of the desired impressions and atmosphere, economy, clarity, force, all that is calculated to ' hold ' and ' stir ' an audience and send it away satisfied and with precisely that new experience which it was the dramatist's object to give them. We mean the whole craft of play-writing, but particularly those parts of it which are peculiar to play-writing, or at least more important in the drama than in other forms of literature.

Discussing technique, we must grant in the theatre the audience whom the dramatist intends to address: Congreve is not a bad craftsman because his plays would bore an audience of Bashi-Bazouks who knew no English; and there are differences of taste and practice in various ages. The " Vice in the Old Play " would not go down now, and was out of date and a jest even in Shakespeare's time. Shakespeare had his own difficulties with audiences; some of his hearers wanted poetry and philosophy, some 'knock-about stuff' and obscene jokes. They were very mixed.

We must also relate an author's work to the requirements of his theatre with regard to duration. The Chinese contemplate with equanimity plays which last for several days ; here we prefer a play to last from two to two-and-a-half hours. This was so in Shakespeare's day as in ours: the later we dine the later we sup, and we do not wish to sup at two in the morning. Local taste and technical canons in China allow one to sleep between the acts. The important thing is that in any theatre the dramatist is a bad technician who causes his audience to sleep during the acts. Having regard to the time-condition imposed by the social habits or the patience of his audience, having regard to all the other requiréments and limits of stage representation, we regard that dramatist as the best technician who most successfully sustains his illusion, and communicates what he wishes to communicate with the maximum of interest and excitement that his subject (in the widest sense) permits. In thinking of the merits of technique we must not confuse them with the merits of subjects, nor forget that a play with great technical merits may bore us because the outlook of the author bores us. The degree in which certain technical gifts are called for will vary according to the kind of play. In certain technical respects—what is roughly called general construction—*Charley's Aunt* is a better play than *Hamlet*. But Shakespeare (leaving out of consideration the depth of his wisdom and the loveliness of his poetic utterance) was not writing a farce. The simple object of the author of *Charley's Aunt* was to produce by surprise, by broad paradox, by comic repetition and the accumulation of entanglements, continuous laughter—just touched by sentiment. The convention of farce allows, and even demands, that the characters of farce should be very simple. Had the author of *Charley's Aunt* begun giving his people an 'inner life,' visualizing their home backgrounds, their ambitions in life, their nocturnal dreams and anxieties, or even paused to think of the probabilities of behaviour in any possible human beings, there would have been no farce. The play succeeded because it was based upon hypotheses which experience shows that an ordinary theatre audience will temporarily accept, and the hypotheses were admirably developed with excellent stage dialogue, excellent movement and excellent rough characterization. *Hamlet* may be less technically perfect in its kind; but its kind, ignoring the fact that Shakespeare based his play upon a play by another man, is such as to make technical perfection far more difficult to accomplish and far less important. Shakespeare could not be content with anything less than whole men; working within the normal limits of time, he was impelled not merely to show his sequence of events in such a way as to keep an audience fascinated with the mere story, but to make that sequence flow inevitably from the nature of his characters, and to exhibit his characters in all their dimensions and with all their faculties, so that we should permanently feel them to be real people; and, showing them thus completely, he had to reconcile their natural relations, interactions, affections and antipathies and impulses with the outline of his plot. Here was a world of work for technique to do (and, sometimes, to fail to compass), for space was limited and the stage has but the speech and action of persons for the conveyance of all things that must be conveyed, whilst the illusion of reality has to be sustained.

Discussing technique, we are really discussing everything by which the dramatist's chosen object is to be secured, from the large architectural construction of his play to the smallest artifices that he employs to secure effects of detail, from his choice of scene to his choice of words: but we are not discussing his mind or his heart, his philosophy, morality, temperament, affections, hatreds or insight into character. Whatever changes of taste and method may be witnessed in the theatre, it will be found that certain governing principles are common to the technique of the drama (in so far as it is effective drama) in all ages.

Before we come closer to an account of the main elements in, and canons of, technique, we may skirmish round the subject by a few illustrations which may throw a preliminary light. Speaking precisely, every word in a play is technically right or wrong; and the word which appears unnatural on the lips of a character, at any rate of a character in a given situation, is a technical error; the word (even though it be but " Hands up! " or " Damn! ") which brings the curtain down amid thunders of applause is a technical triumph. Something will be said of words later on; here we shall confine ourselves to larger aspects of the question, and we shall discover something about it at once if we consider a few " maladies most incident " to plays.

Suppose a play begins—as *Cymbeline* begins—with the people standing about telling each other things we feel they must know already, and patently doing it merely because the author wishes the audience to know those things as a preliminary to his play. We say that this is technically bad, and that the author, if he must start with these facts, had far better start with a detached ' Prologue,' who makes no pretence to be a human being and a character in the play.

Suppose an author has a big emotional climax in his first act and none afterwards; we say he has made a technical mistake, as we do if his central ' feature ' is a mystery and it is fully cleared up long before the end.

Suppose an author interposes a great deal of unrelated conversation at a moment when we are passionately anxious to see a development in action

—or even to get away from the theatre. He is technically in error.

Suppose an author leads us to think that his theme is such and such, and awakes our curiosity as to the sequel to certain events, and then forgets to show us the sequel: his work has a technical flaw.

Suppose a character who has been talking on one plane of reality descends or ascends to another, a lay figure leaping to life or a live character suddenly behaving like a puppet: there is a weakness in technique.

Suppose we feel, after accepting a series of events, that the conclusion of them does not arise naturally from the given characters and circumstances but is forced by the author—whether by way of distortion or premature concatenation—for his own convenience: a technical blunder has been made.

Suppose a crisis for which preparations have been made seems disproportionately tame when it comes: there is bad technique.

Suppose an author has required of a producer or an actor some effect or action that no one can convincingly produce: there is bad technique.

Suppose we feel that a 'point' that has been made has not been taken in, or that characters, to suit the plot, have been dragged to places where they would not have gone, or that they believe things that they could not believe, or that they must have done things which they would not have done, or that they must have had relations with each other which would have made things go differently, or that they are expressing the author's opinions and not their own, or that the author is arbitrarily moving them on and off the stage: there is bad technique.

If we reflect upon all these, or any of a hundred other possible faults in a dramatist, we shall find that every one has a psychological reference to the audience. Either the audience is bored, or its curiosity is awakened and not appeased, or its sense of reality is violated, or it fails to apprehend something that it ought to know, or to see something which the author wants it to see, or its natural expectations are disappointed, or its response to certain combinations has been miscalculated. In some way the dramatist has lost full control over the audience. That full control it is his business to keep.

Every original playwright has, in a sense, a technique of his own; every age, even, generates certain technical devices, of which some may be only ephemerally effective by virtue of their novelty, or their suitability to something in the mentality of their own age. No sensible modern dramatist would cut his knot by a duel in which the two combatants killed each other—not because such an encounter is impossible, but because a modern audience presented with it would at once think of a playwright using a hoary trick and not of two characters killing each other. The first dropped handkerchiefs, the first purloined letters, the first secret panels, were all very much more effective than the last can be. Here we find technique in certain subordinate aspects changing. At this present time, again, a play in thirty scenes (which Shakespeare would freely write, though the printed subdivisions were made by his editors later) is technically unsuited to the theatre because of the elaborateness and expensiveness of modern scenery and the rents of modern playhouses. Shakespeare (who worked in a theatre with a few suggestive curtains, balconies and properties) could present vast panoramas that we cannot, though the time may come for them again. The Age of the Unities could not stand it; the Age of Elaborate Scenery can hardly understand it. Such a scene as *Lear*, II. 3, in which Edgar delivers himself of twenty lines and we are on the heath for almost a minute and a half, does its work of panorama and also gives a necessary effect of passage of time; but (possibly in the main, because of the development of scenery) the construction would not have been passed by a modern writer. *King John*, II. 1, in which three several armies are on the stage and a royal marriage is proposed by a besieged citizen from his ramparts, would also appear awkward to a modern who thought of it; but probably did not in the Elizabethan theatre, where more was habitually left to the imagination. Shakespeare, when he began writing, had an audience still living in the tradition of the morality and mystery stages and very little hampered by scenery: they did not mind Richmond's and Richard's tents standing side by side, and were inured to long, immobile debates. Shakespeare gradually weaned himself from the old crude technique: he bore in mind the trapdoors and inner stages of his own day, but bothered about them little when writing; the theatre, to him, was meant for the play, not the play for the theatre. He grew and was an improver. Yet there are certain general technical principles which appear to be universally true, principles deduced by experience, and founded upon the very nature and conditions of the drama. There are principles and rules governing essential lines of procedure, determining even the subordinate trick or device which may in any particular work be safely employed.

The effects to be produced upon the audience have been indicated above. We may now indicate some of the means whereby a dramatist, so far as he is able, must endeavour to secure those effects. It is a pity, one may add, that Hamlet, with his remarkable clarity of mind and concision of speech, did not make a speech to Playwrights like his speech to the Players. Shakespeare knew (we may be sure) all that was to be known of the art, careless though he often was; and that fluent tongue, of which Jonson complained, must have freely propounded it at the Mermaid.

In his later plays he avoids mistakes that he made in the earlier, and polishes all his dramatic weapons: no such advance in practice could have been made without a sure grasp on theory, by a man who thought about all things. But we look in vain in his plays for the expression of his thoughts on the drama, the most relevant of his references being the joke in *Lear* about Edgar's entrance: " Pat he comes, like the catastrophe of the old comedy."

First of all, a dramatist must know what his subject is to be. " I intended an ode, but it turned to a sonnet," wrote Austin Dobson: well enough so that no traces of the ode remained. Flecker's *Hassan*, parts of which are sufficiently fine to suggest that a potentially great dramatist died with him, suffers from uncertainty in this regard. The first act suggests that a comedy of Hassan is preparing; later we discover the central subject to be a tragedy of Rafi and Pervaneh. We happen to know that the play was originally conceived as a farce and that the first act is all that remains of the original conception. Whatever the explanation of the mixture, the work as we possess it suffers because the later story was not completely substituted for the former: time is wasted and tone has to be changed; and we wonder what of beauty and force might not have been gained had the poet lived to begin his play anew with Pervaneh in her native mountains or Rafi first encountering her in the bazaar, premonitions of the ultimate tragedy in the air from the initial rising of the curtain. Alone of the old unities, the old 'unity of action' has, in a sense, survived all experience. There must be a single story, a dominant theme, to which all else in a play is subservient; a story which, when translated into dramatic terms, is called plot, a pillar around which all that is not itself is garlanded. Unless we can give a compact answer to the question: " What is the play about ? " the play is, in one respect at least, defective, and will miss its effect.

The 'story' having been determined upon, it has to be converted into 'plot.' It has to be presented as a story can most effectively be presented upon the stage: the 'straight' narration of conversation or print thereby suffering all manner of modifications, rearrangements, eliminations, determined by the limitations of the theatre. The 'plot' of a play, if effective, must be very different from the 'story' of a novel, quite apart from the question of length. People are always remarking that it is a mistake to attempt to turn a play into a novel or a novel into a play. The generalization is false. A magnificent novel might be made out of *Hamlet*. But there is fire behind the smoke. The requirements and possibilities of the two arts differ profoundly. In the theatre we have nothing but dialogue between people who must keep moving and doing in a natural way: no delightful digressions or analyses can be a substitute for suspense about what is to happen next; and the author cannot interfere, in his own person, with fine descriptions of gesture, glowing accounts of sunset or storm, or meditations, proper to himself but not to the characters, on life in general. On the stage all must be compressed, all must be naturally spoken in possible conversation or soliloquy; nothing, since nothing can be skipped, must be dull; nothing, since nothing can be recapitulated, must be obscure. The real trouble about translation from one medium to the other is that the translators are usually too much influenced by the order or content before them, endeavouring —unable to endeavour otherwise—to secure in a new medium the old effects in the old ways. Yet, to perceive what a gulf divides the two arts, we have only to take one of Shakespeare's plays and conceive how any great novelist would have treated the theme had Shakespeare never written a play about it.

Consider the story of Hamlet. What novelist in the world, with ' all the time there is ' at his disposal, would have dreamed of plunging his readers *in medias res* with the soldiers on the battlements and the distant appearance of the Ghost? That, if it came, would probably come more than half-way through a novel, which probably would have begun far back, with Hamlet a student at Wittenberg and the first seeds of a guilty passion germinating in the heart of Denmark's Queen. However the book might have begun, with a description of Denmark, or a picture of the young prince riding home from the University, or an account of his first youthful meeting with Ophelia, we may be sure we should have seen much of Hamlet before that midnight on the battlements. This, like the other plays, full though it may be, is but the end of a novel: indeed, one of the chief problems of the serious dramatist is to indicate briefly and easily as he goes all those preliminaries to what he shows, which would have formed a large part of the substance of a novel on his theme. Compare the content of a good play of (say) fifteen thousand words and a short story of the same length. How much more it contains! Compare it with a long novel. How different is the content! A play is *sui generis*. A play has its own manner of beginning, its own manner of conveying information, its own manner of evoking 'atmosphere,' its own requirements as to order, determined by its own necessity for unity, suspense, crescendo and the economic delineation of characters and relations. By the same token, it has advantages of its own, for conveying, by inflections of voice, by facial expressions, by gestures, by physical confrontations and actions, by scenery and lights, by interrupting curtains, much that in a novel needs a flux of words. Seeing, to some extent, is believing.

There is no space here, even were the author capable of its composition, for a manual of dramatic technique; or even for a leisurely approach, step by step, to its principal problem. Those who wish for clear and sensible information on the subject may be commended to the late Professor George P. Baker's *Dramatic Technique* and the late William Archer's *Play-Making*. But it was desirable that we should summarize here some of the difficulties which a dramatist must surmount, and some of the temptations which he must resist: a certain amount having been indicated in the instances, given above, of errors. It will be found that, ultimately, everything depends on the appeal to the chosen audience approached within the necessary playing time. A play (like an advertisement) is an experiment in practical psychology.

And as a concrete example of the sort of work that has to be done and the sort of faults that have to be avoided, we cannot do better than take Professor Baker's instance. He quotes in parallel columns the Hubert and Arthur scene from the old play of *King John* and the scene as Shakespeare rewrote it.

I take the quotations from him bodily, as they illustrate perfectly what happens when a great dramatist and poet gets to work on situations and characters from which none but he could get " full value." The contrast is tremendous, and I only wish that my friend Professor Baker were alive, so that I could acknowledge the debt. He was a really practical theorist who taught many craftsmen their job.

Act IV. Scene I. *Northampton. A Room in the Castle.*

Enter Hubert de Burgh with three men.

Hub.: My masters, I have shewed you what warrant I have of this attempt; I perceive by your heavie countenances you had rather be otherwise imployed, and for my owne part, I would the King had made choyce of some other executioner; onely this is my comfort, that a King commaunds, whose precepts neglected or omitted, threatneth torture for the default. Therefore in brief, leave me, and be readie to attend the adventure: stay within that entry, and when you hear me crie, God save the King, issue sodainly foorth, lay handes on Arthur, set him in his chayre, wherein (once fast bound) leave him with me to finish the rest.

Attendants: We goe, though loath.

(*Exeunt.*)

Hub.: My Lord, will it please your Honour to take the benefite of the faire evening?

Enter Arthur to Hubert de Burgh.

Arth.: Gramercie Hubert for thy care of me,
In or to whom restraint is newly knowen,
The joy of walking is small benefit,
Yet will I take thy offer with small thankes,
I would not loose the pleasure of the eye.
But tell me curteous Keeper if you can,
How long the King will have me tarrie here.

Hub.: I know not Prince, but as I gesse, not long.
God send you freedome, and God save the King.

(*They issue forth.*)

Arth.: Why now sirs, what may this outrage meane?
O helpe me Hubert, gentle Keeper helpe;
God send this sodaine mutinous approach
Tend not to reave a wretched guiltless life.

Enter Hubert and two Attendants.

 Hub.: Heat me these irons hot, and look thou stand
Within the arras: when I strike my foot
Upon the bosom of the ground, rush forth,
And bind the boy, which you shall find with me
Fast to the chair: be heedful. Hence and watch.
 1*st Attend.*: I hope your warrant will bear out the deed.
 Hub.: Uncleanly scruples! fear not you: look to't.
         (*Exeunt Attendants.*)
Young lad, come forth; I have to say with you.
      Enter Arthur.
 Arth.: Good morrow, Hubert.
 Hub.:   Good morrow, little prince.
 Arth.: As little prince (having so great a title
To be more prince) as may be. You are sad.
 Hub.: Indeed, I have been merrier.
 Arth.:   Mercy on me!
Methinks nobody should be sad but I:
Yet I remember, when I was in France
Young gentlemen would be as sad as night,
Only for wantonness. By my christendom,
So I were out of prison and kept sheep,
I should be as merry as the day is long;
And so I would be here, but that I doubt
My uncle practises more harm to me:
He is afraid of me and I of him.
Is it my fault that I was Geffrey's son?
No, indeed, is't not; and I would to heaven
I were your son, so you would love me, Hubert.
 Hub. (*aside*): If I talk to him with his innocent prate

> *Hub.:* So sirs, depart, and leave the rest forme.
> *Arth.:* Then Arthur yeeld, death frowneth in thy face,
>
> What meaneth this? Good Hubert plead the case.
> *Hub.:* Patience young Lord, and listen words of woe,
>
> Harmful and harsh, hells horror to be heard:
> A dismall tale fit for a furies tongue.
> I faint to tell, deepe sorrow is the sound.
> *Arth.:* What, must I die?
> *Hub.:* No newes of death, but tidings of more hate.
>
> A wrathfull doome, and most unluckie fate:
> Deaths dish were daintie at so fell a feast,
> Be deafe, heare not, its hell to tell the rest.
> *Arth.:* Alas, thou wrongst my youth with words of feare,
>
> 'Tis hell, 'tis horror, not for one to heare:
> What is it man if needes be don,
> Act it, and end it, that the paine were gon.
> *Hub.:* I will not chaunt such dolour with my tongue,
>
> Yet must I act the outrage with my hand.
> My heart, my head, and all my powers beside,
> To aide the office have at once denide.
> Peruse this Letter, lines of treble woe,
> Reade ore my charge, and pardon when you know.
> Hubert, these are to commaund thee, as thou tendrest our quiet in minde, and the estate of our person, that presently upon the receipt of our commaund, thou put out the eies of **Arthur Plantaginet.**
> *Arth.:* Ah, monstrous damned **man! his very** breath infects the elements.
>
> Contagious venyme dwelleth in his heart;

He will awake my mercy, which lies dead:
Therefore I will be sudden, and dispatch.
   Arth.: Are you sick, Hubert? you look pale to-day.
In sooth, I would you were a little sick,
That I might sit all night, and watch with you:
I warrant I love you more than you do me.
   Hub. (*aside*): His words do take possession of my bosom.
Read here, young Arthur.
                        (*Showing a paper.*)
             (*Aside*) How now, foolish rheum!
Turning dispiteous torture out of door!
I must be brief, lest resolution drop
Out at mine eyes in tender womanish tears.
Can you read it? Is it not fair writ?
   Arth.: Too fairly, Hubert, for so foul effect.
Must you with hot irons burn out both mine eyes?
   Hub.: Young boy, I must.
   Arth.:   And will you?
   Hub.:   And I will.
   Arth.: Have you the heart? When your head did but ache,
I knit my handkerchief about your brows,
(The best I had, a princess wrought it me)
And I did never ask it you again:
And with my hand at midnight held your head,
And like the watchful minutes to the hour
Still and anon cheer'd up the heavy time,
Saying, 'What lack you?' and, 'Where lies your grief?'
Or, 'What good love may I perform for you?'
Many a poor man's son would have lain still,
And ne'er have spoke a loving word to you;

Effecting meanes to poyson all the world.
Unreverent may I be to blame the heavens
Of great injustice, that the miscreant
Lives to oppress the innocents with wrong.
Ah, Hubert! makes he thee his instrument,
To sound the tromp that causeth hell triumph?
Heaven weepes, the Saints do shed celestiall teares,
They feare thy fall, and cyte thee with remorse,
To knock thy conscience, moving pitie there,
Willing to fence thee from the range of hell,

Hell, Hubert, trust me all the plagues of hell
Hangs on performance of this damned deede.
This seale, the warrant of the bodies blisse,
Ensureth Satan chieftaine of thy soule:
Subscribe not Hubert, give not Gods part away,
I speake not only for eyes priviledge,
The chiefe exterior that I would enjoy:
But for they perill, farre beyond my paine,
Thy sweetes soules losse, more than my eyes vaine lack:
A cause internall, and eternall too,
Advise thee Hubert, for the case is hard,
To loose salvation for a Kings reward.
  Hub.: My Lord, a subject dwelling in the land
Is tyed to execute the Kings commaund.
  Arth.: Yet God commaunds whose power reacheth further,
That no commaund should stand in force to murther.
  Hub.: But that same Essence hath ordained a law,
A death for guilt, to keepe the world in awe.
  Arth.: I pleade, not guiltie, treasonlesse and free.

But you at your sick-service had a prince.
Nay, you may think my love was crafty love,
And call it cunning: do an if you will.
If heaven be pleas'd that you will use me ill,
Why then you must. Will you put out mine eyes?
These eyes that never did, nor never shall
So much as frown on you?
   Hub.:   I have sworn to do it;
And with hot irons must I burn them out.
   Arth.: Ah! none but in this iron age would do it.
The iron of itself, though heat red-hot,
Approaching near these eyes would drink my tears,
And quench this fiery indignation
Even in the matter of mine innocence;
Nay, after that, consume away in rust,
But for containing fire to harm mine eye.
Are you more stubborn-hard than hammered iron?
An if an angel should have come to me,
And told me Hubert should put out mine eyes,
I would not have believ'd him; no tongue but
    Hubert's.
   Hub.: (*Stamps.*) Come forth.
Re-enter Attendants, with Cord, Irons, etc.
Do as I bid you do.
   Arth.: O! save me, Hubert, save me! my eyes are
    out
Even with the fierce looks of these bloody men.
   Hub.: Give me the iron, I say, and bind him here.
   Arth.: Alas! what need you be so boisterous-
    rough?
I will not struggle; I will stand stone-still.
For heaven's sake, Hubert, let me not be bound.
Nay, hear me, Hubert: drive these men away,
And I will sit as quiet as a lamb;

> *Hub.:* But that appeale, my Lord, concernes not me.
> *Arth.:* But thou art he that maist omit the perill.
> *Hub.:* I, if my Soveraigne would remit his quarrell.
> *Arth.:* His quarrell is unhallowed false and wrong.
> *Hub.:* Then be the blame to whom it doth belong.
> *Arth.:* Why thats to thee if thou as they proceede,
> Conclude their judgement with so vile a deede.
> *Hub.:* Why then no execution can be lawfull
> If Judges doomes must be reputed doubtfull.
> *Arth.:* Yes where in forme of Lawe in place and time,
> The offended is convicted of the crime.
>
> *Hub.:* My Lord, my Lord, this long expostulation,
> Heapes up more griefe, than promise of redresse;
> For this I know, and so resolude I end,
> That subjects lives on Kings commaunds depend.
> I must not reason why he is your foe,
> But doo his charge since he commaunds it so.
> *Arth.:* Then doo thy charge, and charged be thy soule
> With wrongfull persecution don this day.
> You rowling eyes, whose superficies yet
> I doo behold with eyes that Nature lent:
> Send foorth the terror of your Moovers frowne,
> To wreake my wrong upon the murtherers,
> That rob me of your faire reflecting view:
> Let hell to them (as earth they wish to me)
> Be darke and direfull guerdon for their guylt,
> And let the black tormenters of deepe Tartary

I will not stir, nor wince, nor speak a word,
Nor look upon the iron angerly.
Thrust but these men away, and I'll forgive you,
Whatever torment you do put me to.
 Hub.: Go, stand within: let me alone with him.
 1st Attend.: I am best pleas'd to be from such a
  deed.
         (*Exeunt Attendants.*)
 Arth.: Alas! I then have chid away my friend:
He hath a stern look, but a gentle heart.—
Let him come back, that his compassion may
Give life to yours.
 Hub.:   Come, boy, prepare yourself.
 Arth.: Is there no remedy?
 Hub.:   None but to lose your eyes.
 Arth.: O heaven! that there were but a mote in
  yours,
A grain, a dust, a gnat, a wandering hair,
Any annoyance in that precious sense!
Then, feeling what small things are boisterous there,
Your vile intent must needs seem horrible.
 Hub.: Is this your promise? go to, hold your
  tongue.
 Arth.: Hubert, the utterance of a brace of tongues
Must needs want pleading for a pair of eyes:
Let me not hold my tongue; let me not, Hubert:
Or Hubert, if you will, cut out my tongue,
So I may keep mine eyes. O! spare mine eyes;
Though to no use, but still to look on you.
Lo! by my troth, the instrument is cold
And would not harm me.
 Hub.:   I can heat it, boy.
 Arth.: No, in good sooth; the fire is dead with
  grief,

Upbraide them with this damned enterprise,
Inflicting change of tortures on their soules.
Delay not, Hubert, my orisons are ended,
Begin, I pray thee, reave me of my sight:
But to performe a tragedie indeede,
Conclude the period with a mortal stab,
Constance farewell, tormenter come away,
Make my dispatch the Tyrants feasting day.

Hub.: I faint, I feare, my conscience bids desist:
Faint did I say? fear was it that I named:
My King commaunds, that warrant sets me free:
But God forbids, and he commandeth Kings,
That great Commaunder counterchecks my charge,
He stayes my hand, he maketh soft my heart.
Goe cursed tooles, your office is exempt,
Cheere thee young Lord, thou shalt not loose an eye,
Though I should purchase it with losse of life.
Ile to the King and say his wille is done,
And of the langor tell him thou art dead,
Goe in with me, for Hubert was not borne
To blinde those lampes that nature polisht so.

Arth.: Hubert, if ever Arthur be in state,
Looke for amends of this received gift,
I tooke my eyesight by thy curtesie,
Thou lentst them me, I will not be ingrate.
But now procrastination may offend
The issue that thy kindness undertakes:
Depart we Hubert, to prevent the worst.
                                            (*Exeunt.*)

Being create for comfort, to be us'd
In undeserv'd extremes: see else yourself;
There is no malice in this burning coal;
The breath of heaven hath blown his spirit out
And strew'd repentant ashes on his head.
   Hub.: But with my breath I can revive it, boy.
   Arth.: An if you do you will but make it blush
And glow with shame of your proceedings, Hubert:
Nay, it perchance will sparkle in your eyes;
And like a dog that is compell'd to fight,
Snatch at his master that doth tarre him on.
All things that you should use to do me wrong,
Deny their office: only you do lack
That mercy, which fierce fire and iron extends,
Creatures of note for mercy-lacking uses.
   Hub.: Well, see to live; I will not touch thine eyes
For all the treasures that thine uncle owes:
Yet am I sworn and I did purpose, boy,
With this same very iron to burn them out.
   Arth.: O! now you look like Hubert; all this while
You were disguised.
   Hub.:   Peace! no more. Adieu.
Your uncle must not know but you are dead;
I'll fill these dogged spies with false reports:
And, pretty child, sleep doubtless and secure,
That Hubert, for the wealth of all the world,
Will not offend thee.
   Arth.:   O heaven! I thank you, Hubert.
   Hub.: Silence! no more, go closely in with me:
Much danger do I undergo for thee.
                                           (*Exeunt.*)

Apart from the fact that one is good poetry and the other is not, notice the deliberate conscious craft of the dramatic artist. How he brings the characters to life! How the waste of words is eliminated! How unerringly he begins with a concrete image and a speech like an action: "Heat me these irons hot," setting the whole scene, instead of long-winded talk! How pity is brought in, and genuine terror, instead of the mere mechanics of horror! How, throughout, every device is employed to make the scene vivid, to amplify its emotional content, to deepen the sense of real conflict! These passages are a manual in themselves.

CHAPTER IV

PLOT, CONSTRUCTION, DEVICE

DR. JOHNSON observed that there was perhaps not one play of Shakespeare's perfect. It would have been odd if there were. For twenty years he averaged two plays a year; he had to earn his living; and when he composed a play, all he had in sight was a brief run, or even possibly a single performance before some royal or noble patron, who certainly would not boggle over a lack of perfection. " The theatre," says Mr. Granville-Barker, " was for Shakespeare a laboratory where he worked—if but in a mimic sense—with human material. His method, his means to enlightenment, was to take a story and put the worth of it, its truth to nature, to the test of personal expression. The story might suffer; if it was not true to nature, it generally would. But Shakespeare was, on the whole, the most unconscientious story-teller, except when history bound him." Moreover, the art was in its infancy when he began. He was a pioneer, both in tragedy and in comedy; English comedy, in fact, he virtually created. He lived in a time when fashion succeeded fashion on the stage, and he adapted himself to every fashion, seldom finding time to write a whole play in the pure light of his own highest conceptions. Finally, like other artists, he developed; and the growth of his powers might be illustrated in a hundred aspects: in such a large thing as his handling of plot, in such a little thing as his idea and use of the clowns whom he took from the mediæval stage. Here, however (particularly since the dates of his plays, as well as his share in some of them, are still uncertain), we shall make it our business to study his main characteristics and achievements rather than his " periods."

Apart from minor flaws (some of which may be textual corruptions) there are, in many of the plays, defects which a more careful, or a less preoccupied, artist would have remedied. " His work," says Mr. Granville-Barker, " abounds in improvisations of technique; he is skilful, and never more skilful than when he is in a difficulty, though often enough even then it is the vitality behind the skill which pulls him through. As to rhetoric, he is capable on occasion of the wantonest use of it and of a little fine sound and fury for its own sake."

Every possible fault in technique can be illustrated (though some very slenderly) from Shakespeare's practice, every kind of triumph of technique can be exampled from it, and in examining what he did by the standard of perfection, we are subjecting him to a test which, had he cared, he might have passed without loss. We may begin with his themes, and his treatment of plot.

The stories of Shakespeare's plays were in almost every instance taken from history books (Plutarch or Holinshed), or from collections of short stories, or

PLOT, CONSTRUCTION, DEVICE

from previously existing plays, themselves drawn from one or other of those sources. His preference for a pre-existing theme offers a very interesting subject for speculation, particularly as it has been shared by most of the great dramatists and narrative poets of the world. The Greek tragedians were content to interpret their myths; few of the stories of Elizabethan tragedy were spontaneously generated. Goethe was content with Faust. Milton, setting out to write an epic, hesitated between Eden and Camelot; he did not think of inventing a story himself, bones, feathers and all. A dramatist seems to be helped when he knows, however slight may be his basis, that he is writing of " things done long ago and ill done "; or at least he finds it easier for his thoughts to crystallize around, and his imagination to spring from, characters already given him. It is even conceivable that most men can give more credence to stories presented to them from outside than to stories fabricated by themselves, of whose artificiality they are acutely aware. However that may be, it will be found that the nature of the materials with which he worked gave Shakespeare the opportunity for some of his superbest achievements, and also accounted for some of his particular failures.

Historical themes have their own particular difficulties and advantages. If the audience already knows anything of the subject, it will want to be shown what it knows (*e.g.* a play, however exciting, about King Harold which did not end with Hastings would be very disappointing) and, rather than miss what it expects, it will suffer a great deal of discontinuity, bad proportion and discursively panoramic treatment. Moreover, it is peculiarly fascinated by anything which it is told really happened: it is a pleasure to see the things that we have read about come to life; it is like living in the past; and we do not mind if we do it in sections. Thomas Hardy's *The Dynasts* has, in print, a spirit and a thread which bind its *disjecta membra*: a great era and a great struggle stand as symbols of all human periods and strifes, and the eternal fates, ironies and pities brood over all. When a greatly reduced version—very cunningly made by Mr. Granville-Barker—was put upon the London stage, the sense of unity and progress was largely lost; yet it was delightful to watch the successive episodes—British volunteers lighting a beacon on the coast, Nelson dying in Hardy's arms, Lord Uxbridge having his leg shot off: a sort of Pathé News Gazette of a hundred years ago. To that extent the historical dramatist's task is lightened. It remains true that, in so far as he is able to epitomize history as a background for central figures, he will make more exciting plays, and also that, presented with a great mass of incident and event that demands representation, he is apt to find his means inadequate. Of this last difficulty Shakespeare—than whom no man ever had a greater gift for suggesting great spaces, times and multitudes by significant detail—was acutely aware. In the prologue

PLOT, CONSTRUCTION, DEVICE 63

to the fifth, first and third acts of *Henry V* he addresses the audience:

> Vouchsafe to those that have not read the story,
> That I may prompt them: and of such as have,
> I humbly pray them to admit the excuse
> Of time, of numbers, and due course of things,
> Which cannot in their huge and proper life
> Be here presented.

And:

> Think when we talk of horses that you see them
> Printing their proud hoofs i' the receiving earth;
> For 'tis your thoughts that now must deck our kings. . . .

And:
>   O! do but think
> You stand upon the rivage and behold
> A city on the inconstant billows dancing;
> For so appears this fleet majestical,
> Holding due course to Harfleur.

The modern realistic theatre would show it all: the poetical drama has died with scenery and the failure to appeal to the audience's imagination.

Another difficulty of the historical drama is here indicated: exposition which the educated part will resent or be fatigued by is very necessary for the uneducated part, who hardly know Harry of Monmouth from Alexander of Macedon. It may be also remarked that Shakespeare proceeds to pour out through the mouth of the chorus a great mass of exposition for which he has not room in his play—the whole narrative of the King's return to England, his welcome there, and then his journey back to France. Had Henry been an imaginary king, Shakespeare the dramatist would have conveyed any essentials there may be in this through the ordinary medium of dialogue; the rest he would have suppressed. *Macbeth*, in a sense (taken out of Holinshed) had a historical basis; but the story and its figures were remote and vague, and, for dramatic purposes, Shakespeare twisted the legend in all sorts of ways. He made Duncan good instead of bad; he caused him to be killed in Macbeth's castle; he blackened Macbeth; Lady Macbeth as we have her is virtually his creation. But known history, unfortunately, must not be too much distorted for the purposes of drama. The informed audience will not stand it: not only is the end, but most of the main events are, predestined. If the characters, as they take shape under the pen, will not fit the predestined plot, so much the worse for the characters; and if the course of events will not allow of due prominence being given to the most interesting characters, so much the worse for the play.

Nevertheless, there is a wide range of choice for the dramatist, and it is very informing to compare the handling of those historical plays in which (on grounds having no relation to construction) Shakespeare is allowed to have had little hand with that of those which are undoubtedly his. The three parts of *Henry VI* and *Henry VIII* are patently, to anyone with any sense of character, morality and style, in the main not Shakespeare's. By the same token we discover that they are dramatically very defective. In *Henry VI* the authors, if they were holding the mirror up to nature, must have been holding it up to the Wars of the Roses: the play has the same vagrant, discrete, wearily fluctuating, uncentred air. Characters are made transiently interesting and dropped again; there are moments of true Shakespeare, but they do not bring the true Shakespeare sequels; Henry VI (a character after Shakespeare's own heart) is once beautifully shown, but is otherwise only one amongst the miscellaneous peregrinating ruck of dukes and earls. When we are listening to Gloucester (whose part is an obvious preparation for *Richard III*), we hear the sustained voice of Shakespeare and feel what he would have done with that play, for all the historical difficulties, had he written it all himself. *Henry VIII*, by the same token, is one of the worst-shaped plays that ever was put upon the stage—redeemed by its fine passages and its pageantry. Had every line satisfied the syllable counters (who note Fletcher[1] everywhere) as being Shakespeare's, the construction would still have given us pause. What is the theme ? At the beginning we might have thought it

[1] Long before I knew anybody had breathed so heretical a suggestion I had formed the opinion that Shakespeare may well have begun a *Henry VIII* in Elizabeth's time—and then found that Tudors on the stage would be too dangerous, and held the manuscript over, to be ultimately dragged on, out of shape, enlarged, and ornamented by Fletcher, when Elizabeth was safely underground.

the tragedy of Catherine of Aragon, with the figures of Henry and the Cardinal as her opposites, the Cardinal being synchronously ruined by the remorseless King who, in the end, has discarded both, the old wife and the old servant. But no. The Cardinal dies. Catherine dies. Buckingham, quite incidentally, dies—perhaps no play can properly be ranked as an English historical play in which somebody called Buckingham does not get killed. And then the play sails on to Anne Boleyn, a happy marriage, a happy childbirth, Cranmer, cheering crowds, and a characterless Henry desperately whitewashed. Anyone strongly moved by the first part of the play would wish Henry to be punished. Since history does not permit of that, a sensible playwright would obviously have dropped the curtain when the tragedy of Catherine and Wolsey had been worked out. Instead of that the invertebrate thing sprawls on, relying on costumes and physical movement for its hold; without a theme, without a hero, without a designated villain, without an end, happy or unhappy, and leaving us with so dim a picture of Henry VIII that it does not even pretend to displace or supplement the conception we have drawn from other sources.

Shakespeare's two Richards and his Henry V, in so far as they diverge from historical truth, have supplanted it, so vivid are they. And their vividness is partly due to the construction of the plays in which they figure. They are in the centre of the picture, their fortunes are the dramatist's theme, and (in

PLOT, CONSTRUCTION, DEVICE 67

varying degrees) all his resources are used to command our interest in them. The result is that we are far more concerned about the fate of Richard II than we are about that of Henry VI, who not merely was a better and tenderer man, but is actually shown to be so in the plays. And the mere figure of Henry V is the making of his play, which, in a general way, is slackly constructed, and lacking in any, save physical, conflict.

But among the historical plays undoubtedly mainly written by Shakespeare there is a considerable difference of handling. *King John* is not one of the best. Arthur, one of the two really sympathetic figures, is not sufficiently in the centre of the picture. *His* tragedy, as the theme of a whole play, might perhaps have been too uselessly painful; but Shakespeare, had he not based his work on a pre-existing play, might have taken it for his theme. The alternative (since the bastard Fauconberg could hardly have commanded the stage) was to make John and his fate interesting, which Shakespeare, unimpeded, was quite capable of doing. The play, as it stands, leaves an impression of shapelessness and lack of direction: it is like a series of slices from a chronicle. To see how Shakespeare really could work it is perhaps best to take, not those plays —the *Richards* and *Henry V*—in which he subordinated all to one dominating figure and kept us hanging on his lips, but those—namely the two parts of *Henry IV*—in which history demanded a considerable discursiveness of action (if the chronicle of events were to be shown at all) and in which the normally leading character, Henry, could not be made either sinister or heroic. The purely humdrum historical part, the marches and plots and battles and preparations for battle, have a swing and suspense about them, an interest and excitement, utterly lacking in *Henry VI*. One event follows hard upon another, and every character introduced, down to Harry Hotspur's wife, engages us. The thing has come to life and been given more of a centre. Shakespeare achieved this much; but feeling even at that, that for the purposes of the stage the sprawling chronicle of Henry Bolingbroke was not as interesting as the chronicle of Richard III, he invented Falstaff and his immortal gang, linked them to the main action via the Prince of Wales, the Chief Justice and military service, and thereby gave the action just that element that holds us breathless until all is done. How deliberately and impudently he did this, and how little pains he took to perfect his structure, is proved by the fact that all the Falstaff scenes will detach bodily and make a self-contained play.

The ancient historical plays Shakespeare handled with varying degrees of success. *Titus Andronicus* is very little his: if we do not saddle him with the preposterous and disgusting plot, and the weak verse, we can hardly perhaps credit him with the splendid melodramatic hustle of it, the unimpeded rattling movement that so transforms it on the stage. *Coriolanus* is an excellently made play;

arguably the best made of all, a play moving firmly from start to finish, organic, developing to an inevitable close, utterly believable, free from waste matter, arousing no conjectures as to incidents or relations undisclosed. Even the battle-scenes before Corioli are dramatically excellent, though possibly awkward to handle in the modern theatre. The play's handicap lies in the absence of sympathetic characters; Coriolanus himself, for all his courage, resolution and pride, irritates us a little, and that is all; nobody that we care for either suffers or succeeds; even his old mother is such a harridan that we do not mind how much she is hurt. It is differentiated from the other great tragedies by the fact that it awakens no pity; it also contains less sheer poetry than they: its fate should be contemplated by those who talk as though 'technique' were the *sole* foundation of dramatic power. The stage exposition of the fable, however, is almost perfect. The grossly misnamed *Julius Cæsar* is also well made: it is the tragedy of Brutus the Whig, and the figure stands out, though much background is revealed and much ground travelled; the plot moves and steadily: it 'grips,' and it is not competed with. There remain *Troilus and Cressida* and *Antony and Cleopatra*, both panoramic war-plays with a tragic love story in the foreground. One of these plays is continually revived. The other is scarcely ever played: why?

Reasons, no doubt, are more than one. The 'serpent of old Nile,' in death as in life, has an immeasurably greater fascination than Cressida, 'the daughter of the game,' a mere light, laughing, provocative, unmalevolent, short-memoried wanton, with nothing but lowered eyelids and a flirted foot to set against the spell cast by the least shrug of Cleopatra's shoulders, the least gesture of her arm or turn of her head; nothing but chatter to compete with the tigerish anger, the languorous yielding, the mysterious conjuration of all the highest as well as all the lowest aspirations of spirit and sense of Cæsar's and Antony's Egypt; Egypt the dark and seductive, who dropped the pearl in the wine, who lay back voluptuously in her barge while the peacock feathers fanned slowly to and fro, who conquered her conquerors with a wave of her jewelled hand, who, crooning, drew the asp to her breast, and died like a lover, a soldier, a martyr and a saint. Antony too—but that brings us precisely to the point. There is no intrinsic reason why Antony should be more interesting than Troilus. Quite the reverse: Shakespeare was tied to an historical Antony, weak, intermittently indolent, faithless, as well as bold, whereas his own Troilus, brave and sensitive boy, contains as he comes to us all the elements of a great tragic hero. But these elements are not all developed. The action of *Antony and Cleopatra* changes from Egypt to Rome, from Rome to Misenum, from Misenum to Egypt, from Egypt to Actium, from Actium to Egypt again. We are shown the Triumvirs; we are shown the pact with Pompey's son; we are shown all the fluctuations of the suspicious armed truce and of the war by land and sea until Octavius' ultimate conquest: yet structurally there is a centre, Antony and Cleopatra, and the play as a stage play is the stronger for it. If Shakespeare felt a temptation to give at least some indication of what the population of Egypt thought and felt and looked like, he resisted it. The royal precincts are all we see during our long sojourn in Egypt, and all the Egyptians are some maids, some slaves—mere attendants all—a soothsayer who says little, and a sketchy peasant who brings in the asp.

In *Troilus and Cressida* Shakespeare never seems quite to have made up his mind what the play was about. In retrospect we remember Troilus and Cressida no more clearly than Thersites and Patroclus, and if we have a dominant impression at all, it is that of the long war between the Greeks and Trojans, approaching its culmination, with Trojans debating within the walls, and Ulysses, Ajax, Agamemnon, Achilles and the rest, all magnificently characterized and all characterized to no dramatic purpose, conferring and disputing without. In no play of Shakespeare is there firmer or more varied characterization (almost entirely male); in none is the dialogue better, or a panoramic effect more surely secured; in none (save only two or three) are there more magnificent speeches or a greater wealth of sheer poetry. Yet, compared with his own finest plays, it fails on the stage and even in the study; and the reason for this is to be found in this uncertainty as to the theme, this glorious wealth of preparation for no very notable climax, this absence of steady movement, this inability to concentrate on something central, and to sacrifice, at whatever cost, the excrescences. Or if the play be first and foremost panoramic (and a panoramic 'subject' is possible, provided the subject be clear), here there are Troilus and Cressida in the centre, inadequate as central supports: we feel that the play might almost have been improved by their omission.

The Trojan War was a temptation. He had begun with Troilus and Criseyde, whom he found in Chaucer; there was no historical Cressida, she was merely a verbal corruption of Briseis, Achilles' captive. As history sometimes tempted or otherwise hampered Shakespeare in the construction of his plays, so also did the stories which he took ready made from previous playwrights or Italian novelists, though his genius was so tremendous that he usually succeeded in obscuring the fact.

Sir Arthur Quiller-Couch tells the story of a sailor in the gallery at a performance of *Othello* who suddenly shouted at a critical moment: "But, you great black fool, don't you see?" The sailor was quite right. He might also, quite as justifiably, have shouted to Desdemona: "Why don't you tell him you have lost your handkerchief?" and to Emilia: "Why didn't you intervene a few minutes before?"—as he might have been astonished at that death from suffocation which permits a temporary recovery and speech.

Shakespeare's Othello (apart from the fact that Shakespeare, lapsing from his highest standards, does not give Desdemona time and opportunity to commit misconduct) ought to have seen; would have seen; and in any event would not have murdered his beloved. Had he really been wrought, on such evidence, to such a pitch of madness, he would have been much more liable to kill himself than to stifle Desdemona's last poor protestations of innocence and affection, subsequently describing himself as:

> one not easily jealous, but, being wrought,
> Perplex'd in the extreme.

Why then did he do it? The reason was that he did it in Shakespeare's original, the Italian Cinthio's story. The trouble is that in that story Othello was not Shakespeare's Othello at all. As Miss Bradbrook says in her fascinating little book, *Elizabethan Stage Conditions*:

> The value of the study of literary sources has been assailed again and again, from Croce to Wilson Knight. The direct application may be of little use, but as a means of measuring the way in which the author's interests work by enabling us to see where he has modified and where he has merely absorbed, much knowledge is a most necessary critical weapon. It may also serve an elucidatory purpose by explaining irrelevancies and inconsistencies which result from an assumption of certain facts that are contained in the sources but not carried over by the work. This is especially likely to happen when a dramatist uses old theatrical material.

Shakespeare's was, as a tragic plot should be, a far simpler and solider plot than Cinthio's. And the old Othello was a far coarser Moor, who went so far as to plot Desdemona's death in conjunction with Iago, and to get her killed in such a way (by battering her with a stocking full of sand) as would enable him to pretend afterwards that the top of her bed had fallen on her; and whose subsequent relations with Iago (whose vile lust for Desdemona Shakespeare also eliminated—presumably for her sake) were those of cunning blackmailer and cunning blackmailee. There was the story: and when the noble Othello, one of the finest and most lovable of men, leapt to life in Shakespeare's brain, he could not be denied, but he had to be fitted into the Procrustean bed of the predetermined plot; to have made him laugh, call Iago a liar, clap him in irons and go home and tell Desdemona, would not have been at all to the purpose. There was, unfortunately, all the difference in the world between an Italian novel and a play of Shakespeare's, and when Shakespeare's breeding mind got to work on an Italian novel, the result was not seldom that his live characters had to be unnaturally forced to behave as the Italian puppets had behaved.

The same thing happened with *The Merchant of Venice*. The bond perhaps may be swallowed, if not the law court which would enforce it. The caskets could be accepted where the lady involved the shadowy lay-figure of an anecdote, but not when a Portia, endowed with flesh, blood, spirit, wisdom and independence by Shakespeare, is involved. Nobody who listened to Portia for one minute can suppose that, whatever happened about the caskets, she would have married the County Palatine, or Monsieur le Bon, or the English "dumb-show," or the drunken nephew of the Duke of Saxony, or that Prince of Morocco to whom she *sotto voce* bid a " gentle riddance." The *Much Ado* story—though it matters less, since we have Beatrice and Benedick—is in the same case. The slander on Hero, and Claudio's subsequent crass conduct, might have been well enough in a few pages of Boccaccio or such another; but as soon as Shakespeare has created his Hero we resent it, and as soon as Claudio believes the slander, we heartily wish Hero rid of him. The objection to the end of *Measure for Measure* stands on another footing: it certainly revolts and disappoints us, and (consequently) is flat in the theatre—but it might conceivably have happened, granted the characters.

Boccaccio himself was the origin of *All's Well that Ends Well*, on which the first comment must be that all is not well, and that it does not end well. Ladies and gentlemen taking refuge in a country garden from the Florentine plague might well be content with such a tale, with all the characters merely 'a certain lady' or 'a certain lord' or 'Messer so-and-So,' and characterized no further than the mechanics of the brief anecdote might render necessary. But here again the very exuberance and veracity of Shakespeare's creative powers handicapped him as a dramatist—since he was too lazy to modify his plot (and he may arguably have been working in collaboration here) to suit the characters he had generated. 'A certain lady' may have cured the King of France of a disease that had defied the doctors, and might have demanded of him as reward the hand of a young nobleman who had scarcely deigned to look at her. She might even have humbled herself so far as to play the trick by which Helena ultimately secured her husband. But not Shakespeare's Helena, so wise and sensitive and proud and percipient and noble, except at the moments when the plot is compelling her to do something unnatural. Here, as in *Measure for Measure*, some of the verse is as un-Shakespearean as the sentiments: according as we think our ears attuned to his voice or our minds to his way of thinking, so shall we judge much in this work that is disputable, which means much more than is commonly disputed. These two plays (and *Troilus*) date from the period of Shakespeare's great tragedies—and of Marston's successes. They are more 'sexual,' in the sense of the modern 'sex-play,' than is Shakespeare's wont. That Shakespeare was working in collaboration with a man who was determined to supply the markets with the unpleasantness it wanted is not beyond possibility.

A forcing of the main plot is also evident in other places where a little trouble, a little retrospective revision, which Shakespeare would not bother to make, would have rendered it unnecessary. *Othello*

PLOT, CONSTRUCTION, DEVICE

would have been a totally different play had Shakespeare shrunk from forcing his conclusion. But no great ingenuity would have been required so to alter the plot of *Lear* as to abolish the need for Edmund's sudden and utterly faked and unconvincing repentance, the repentance, purely for the slack dramatist's convenience, of an inhuman monster. A little thought too might have better prepared the end of *As You Like It*. It is impossible to believe in Oliver's sudden regeneration and the usurper's sudden conversion at the sight of an " old religious man." Here, however, it matters very little. The aim throughout has been fantastic and removed from the everyday: we are in such a happy woodland humour that we forgive the tyranny of mechanics over character. Frustration of another sort, though it be a very minor instance, occurs at the end of *Lear*, where, after the shock of piteousness has passed, we remember one thread that still hangs loose: the gallant King of France who loved Cordelia and took her dowerless, now forgotten, he and his whereabouts and feelings, by Cordelia and by Shakespeare. And to some minds (perhaps not to others) Shakespeare's revision of the old *Shrew* play would have been rounded off more perfectly had we heard a word or two of Sly at the end of it.

Some one fault or flaw may be found in the plots of most of the plays. Where he is not handicapped by history or original tale, it is often a previous play that hampers him. *Hamlet* is a signal instance of this. It is crowded with faults. There are scenes which lead nowhere and the main theme is very confusingly handled. The pretended madness, a legacy, was no longer necessary when the informative ghost was invented, and a world of ingenuity has been expended on efforts to reconcile irreconcilable clues to Hamlet's state of mind and course of thought, all based on the assumption—doubtless a tribute to Shakespeare—that he was a real person, just as enthusiasts treat the events and characters in *Edwin Drood* as real and fully discoverable. All the arguments about superfluous scenes and puzzling psychology would take a different colour were it perpetually remembered that the play as we have it is new wine in an old bottle, that a new Hamlet has to fit an old plot, and that certain passages are retained either because they had already been successful in the theatre, or because Shakespeare was too slack, or thought he could not afford the time, to mend them. The dramatic flaws are usually explicable on such grounds as these. The indisputable plays and passages of Shakespeare justify us in saying that his dramatic sense was unerring if his dramatic practice was not; and that where he works freely he makes his stories plausible growths from his characters, develops them in such a way as to keep us excited, and ends them in a workmanlike and satisfactory manner. His 'underplots' too are usually adequately linked with his main plots, and usually act upon them and are acted on by them. The degree of closeness with which plots are interwoven differs according to the nature of the plays.

In an intense tragedy, which keeps us in an agony of curiosity and concern, we cannot bear a sub-plot which seriously interrupts—at least after the story has really begun to move—the progress of the main plot. The 'play within a play' in *Hamlet* would be intolerable were it not intimately linked with the main plot, a lever to precipitate the crisis. The 'play within a play' in *A Midsummer-Night's Dream* is, dramatically, mere delightful padding: there it doesn't matter, the main plot is too thin to last, the play is a 'dream,' its vagrancy and variety are a part of its charm. Ten minutes of Falstaff and his ragged regiment is a delightful relief in *Henry IV*: in *Lear* it would be an intolerable interruption, or, if not, would seriously diminish the spell cast upon us by the spectacle of the raving King. If there be a sub-plot in *Lear*, it is the plot in which Gloucester and his sons are involved: a thing so interlinked with the main narrative that it is barely separable from it. *Lear* is at one pole. *As You Like It* is at the other. Here much greater liberty was permissible, so Shakespeare took much greater liberty. The interest is sustained, but the suspense is of a temperate kind: the enchantment of the play lies largely in its setting, in the fresh airs that wander through its glades, the babble of brooks, the sense of shy deer behind the trees, the delicious light dialogue of the Arcadian characters. Plot there is: Orlando must win his Rosalind and the Duke must come to his own again; but the course of true love runs very nearly smooth, we never have any doubts about the Duke, and (in any event) the Duke in sylvan exile seems to be having a much more agreeable time than the usurper in his castle. The result is that we are ready for any 'side-show,' willing to be taken down any bypath for a saunter for which there is ample time: and Shakespeare wanders as he feels inclined, with impunity. The speeches go leisurely—what need is there for the 'snap' and 'click'?—and the Audrey-Touchstone story is introduced for its own sake, its sole pretended justification being that it happens, to use Rowe's stage direction, in 'another part of the forest.' It is always just possible, of course, that these, and other characters elsewhere, were afterthoughts introduced to suit particular members of the theatrical company. Everyone now agrees that Shakespeare wrote 'leads' for his 'stars'; and it seems clear that for years he arranged for two boy-heroines, one tall, one short. He was not above dropping in short scenes for the minor 'comic turns' without overmuch concern about the close weaving of his texture.

The strictest sect of modern technicians would hardly find room for this Touchstone and Audrey in any part of the forest. People must not be introduced for their own sakes. These Colins and Peggies must be related to the main action: they should, and naturally, influence the fortunes of Orlando and the Duke; and their intrusion must be 'motivated.' Anything is better than 'the closet drama,' and only a man with a firm grasp on the normal requirements of the stage should attempt the abnormal possibilities. Yet, however some may boast of the triumphs of modern 'construction' (often with shoddy materials), it is difficult not to feel, when surveying the ample prospects of Shakespeare, that we have lost something by rendering impossible the twenty-scene play, by asking for the same close texture in all types of play, by asking of everything (think of the celestial interruption in *The Tempest*!): 'What does it do?' 'Is it motivated?' 'Does it hold up the action?' and 'Could it be compressed?' Shakespeare's liberty sometimes led to licence; but what should we not have lost had he been as severe about essentials and non-essentials as the moderns (always excepting Mr. Bernard Shaw) tend to be? He contrived as it was to give a reflection of life, in its copiousness, variety and waywardness, whilst also keeping a close eye on the requirements of the theatre: the modern drama usually holds either a distorting or a diminishing mirror up to nature, and one reason of that is the cramping produced by a too wholehearted concentration on the dictates, especially the ephemeral dictates, of dramatic theory. But so sure was Shakespeare's hand as a rule, so incapable was he of the major mistakes, that (as has been said) the construction alone must (we instinctively feel) rule out such a play as *Henry VIII* from his canon. The voice is recognizable in an artist's structure as well as in his sentences. How could the deviser of the undisputed plays have been contented with the crude construction of *Timon*: a play of two halves, one before, one after, Timon's ruin, the first exhibiting very little movement, the second none whatever, but a mere static undramatic set of variations on the misanthropic theme, with new characters introduced for the sake of new characters, but modifying things not at all?

There are a few fine Shakespearean passages in the play; but what a gulf divides the mind behind most of it from the mind behind *Coriolanus*, not to mention *Hamlet*! It is the crude psychology of the fabulists, Æsop among the bipeds. Timon is an ass in his faith and an ass in his disillusionment; the rest (yes, even Apemantus, to whom Shakespeare may have done something) are puppets, as none in *Troilus* are puppets, and none in any of the generally accepted plays. And this jellyfish of a play has subsidiary faults not found in such numbers elsewhere, not conceivable in a play made by that wisest of men and most cunning (though careless) of artists. What was that gold that Timon dug up? Shakespeare could never leave a thing like that unexplained, though he might pass it in a work to which he was merely giving a 'lick-over.' The construction of this whole play is weak: there is little development, the situations are meagre, the faint interest which attaches to the Steward is all that gives us a touch of really interesting conflict; the end is crude. The fifth scene of the third act is the oddest of all. Alcibiades is to be brought back as an enemy to Athens (though he need not be, so far as the tragedy of Timon is concerned) so that he should be shown quarrelling with Athens. He does it at great length and on most bewildering grounds, introducing 'a friend of mine' (whom any audience schooled in the theatre might well suppose to be Timon or someone else who is largely involved in the main plot) who has 'outstepp'd the law.' It is never explained who this friend was, nor what precisely his breach; the friend has nothing to do with the play; and all that is needed in this scene to prepare for Alcibiades' not very much needed return would be a line or two of allusive, retrospective dialogue—no more than a Fortinbras has. Faulty as Shakespeare sometimes was, an observance of the elementary laws of the drama may safely be made one test of the authenticity of the doubtful plays; and, significantly, it will be found that, judged by this test, just those plays fail which the metrists question on metrical grounds and the verbalists on grounds of diction. Those who judge instinctively by what seems to them the presence or absence of the speaking, thinking, laughing, suffering Shakespeare have no footing in so scientific an assembly. But they may laugh last.

Flaws in subsidiary details of plot and presentation may, it is true, be found in Shakespeare, but on no impressive scale, save only in those plays in which his share was palpably small. Even minor 'loose ends' are few in the major plays. "When," as it has been aptly said, "he is intensely interested in the theme of a play, tragic or comic, his energy kindles and he spares no trouble to present the story to most complete advantage and to get out of it all that can be expressed from it." In reading *Macbeth* we may feel that Lady Macbeth's " taking-off " is a little sudden, and that the accession difficulty at the end of the second act is rather skated over; on the stage these hasty jumps to a conclusion are not noticeable. Friar Lawrence's rapid exit on hearing a watch coming is unconvincing: though here we have a worked-over play. In *Coriolanus*, I. 6, the mechanism whereby Shakespeare gives Cominius' reactions to good and bad news is rather clumsy. *Hamlet* has many flaws of construction (faulty order of events, faulty psychological sequences; Hamlet at one point unconvincingly forgets his revenge) which, unlike most of Shakespeare's defects, have been discussed *ad nauseam*. An instance less often discussed than the puzzling state of Hamlet's mind (because it is not a matter of wrong order, or irreconcilable facts, or unconvincing psychology) is the first scene of the second act, in which Polonius' long talk with Reynaldo about Laertes in Paris (and Laertes had had quite enough advice from Polonius before he set out for the place) looks as though it were giving a lead to something—but does not. This, as we have said above, may be accounted for as a remainder from the old play; we must mention it, however, as there is no general agreement as to what precisely Shakespeare wrote, what he rewrote, and what he took over bodily. There is a slight awkwardness of construction in *Julius Cæsar* where

Brutus and his friends, with Antony, who has entered, are for so long left alone with Cæsar's body, none of those who fled returning—and this before the Capitol at Rome. The last scene in the third act of *Cymbeline*, though brief, is quite superfluous. The confession of the Queen is absurdly unconvincing. The vision in *Cymbeline*, V. 4, is wanton digression, but no man alive will persuade me that the villainous verse of it is Shakespeare's; the play was not printed until the Folio, and we cannot say what was done to the text.

> *Sici.:* No more, thou thunder-master, show
>   Thy spite on mortal flies:
> With Mars fall out, with Juno chide,
>   That thy adulteries
>   Rates and revenges.
> Hath my poor boy done aught but well,
>   Whose face I never saw?
> I died whilst in the womb he stay'd
>   Attending nature's law:
> Whose father then—as men report,
>   Thou orphans' father art—
> Thou shouldst have been, and shielded him
>   From this earth-vexing smart.

Shakespeare can hardly be saddled with that series of metrical gags.

The end of *The Winter's Tale* is forced and flat. Hermione has to be brought round. From a woman full of character and eloquence she becomes a docile stick, simply for Shakespeare's convenience. Such superfluities as the conversation in the second part of *Henry IV*, IV, 4, a drag on the drama, may be explained by the desire of the contemporary public to obtain historical education as well as dramatic excitement from chronicle plays, for a decade ' the rage.' A close scrutiny of the whole of the plays will discover a few more weak or unnecessary scenes as well, be it understood, as a great many which, according to the modern convention, might be dispensed with or amalgamated with others. In his early stages Shakespeare was not merely a worker on other men's plays, but was still ' learning his job ' in the infancy of the art: the student of his early plays will mark a steady advance in construction, in movement, in the distribution of emphasis and the incorporation of expository matter, and also in characterization. The pruning of unnecessary scenes was one amongst many arts that he mastered. Yet few they are amongst so many. In authentic mature Shakespeare, as a rule, there are few scenes which are not at once worth their place for their own sake and indispensable because of their contribution towards the general movement of the plot. In the longer plays the many scattered scenes are, as it were, tributaries pouring all their water into the main stream that races ever more swiftly until it falls over the steep declivity of the catastrophe.

Shakespeare's resourcefulness and power as a writer for the stage could amply be illustrated by a study of the mere beginnings of his plays. The beginning of a play has various functions—ignoring the pseudo-beginnings of some modern plays, the object of which is to mark time while late ticket-holders are taking their seats. Intrinsically a beginning should seize and keep our attention, by sheer beauty, by surprise, by presenting some brisk action already begun which carries us along in its current, by enveloping us in an air of mysterious expectancy. But, as a rule, the very opening of a play has to carry the burden of necessary exposition —and there was more to be done in an age of no programmes and little scenery. It has to tell us where we are, and give us preliminary information about the persons in the story about to be presented, their situation and their intentions. In Shakespeare's day—he lived during the decay of, and assisted the process of transition from, the mediæval plays—various methods of giving exposition, dumb-show, chorus, soliloquy, were tolerated which are no longer the vogue. To-day the general practice is to give necessary exposition in the dialogue itself. When this is done badly we have the awkward feeling that characters are talking unnaturally in order to inform us; when it is done well information seems to leak out, as it were incidentally, during natural, indeed inevitable, conversation. From Shakespeare's works we may gather a variety of superbly successful examples, and some feebler ones.

A dodge commonly employed by amateur dramatists is the arrival of someone who has been long away and has to be informed as to what has happened in his absence. A weak, outmoded, but not yet entirely discarded trick used for doing this is the production of two servants sweeping and dusting, who talk about the affairs of their masters, who could scarcely do it themselves. The first few times this trick no doubt seemed natural and even delightful, for servants do talk in life; nothing could be more agreeable than Shakespeare's use of the device at the opening of the first act of the *Taming of the Shrew*. But the time came when it seemed that butlers, footmen and other conversable menials were, like dukes and whiskies-and-sodas, even more plentiful on the stage than off, and at once the device became tedious. At best a mere conversation (even when it has more verisimilitude than that at the beginning of *Cymbeline* when the two gentlemen tell each other what they must surely know already), which we know to be put in merely for the purpose of informing us, may seem awkward, and must waste time. The informative conversation at its best and most natural is seen **at the** beginning of *Much Ado*, where the ingenious **stratagem** is used of a messenger who arrives just ahead of the returning Don Pedro and his company. The messenger is able to tell Leonato and his family about Benedick, Claudio and the wars, and Leonato is forced by Beatrice's sprightly sallies to reveal the relations between her and Benedick, the known imminence of Don Pedro's and Benedick's return giving the whole the desirable suspense. This messenger dodge, often used, would become annoying. Here it seems natural for a dignitary like Don Pedro to have his herald riding ahead of him. In all such matters the dramatist is safe if the audience, asking itself why such and such things are being done, does not instantly or instinctively feel that it is " for the author's convenience." The ideal opening informs us in the very act of presenting movement which is structurally part of the plot, and not mere business (like the waiting housewife's titivation of the china-dresser so frequent in bucolic and proletarian dramas) patently devised purely in order to give characters something to do whilst they are producing an inventory of background facts.

How servants can be used is seen in the beginning of *Romeo and Juliet*. There is, it is true, a so-called prologue (possibly not by Shakespeare) which is quite superfluous. Sampson and Gregory appear armed in the streets; since they are liable to meet Montagu's armed servants, they quite naturally talk about them. Abraham and Balthasar then appear and there is the excellent thumb-biting exchange; within a few score lines we pass from servants to Benvolio and Tybalt, then to the heads of the houses, characters appearing in brisk accumulation; a small fight has grown into a general fray, and then the prince has an obvious chance of intervening, quelling the uproar and supplementing our knowledge. The stage has been set for the loves of the enemies' children, we know the whole background against which the tragedy will be enacted; yet all has been done while our blood has been quickened by the swift cut and thrust, the swelling uproar, the sudden pacification by authority. The opening of *The Tempest* again is magnificent. The curtain goes up on a ship at sea, lightning flashing, thunder cracking. A Ship-master and a Boatswain enter:

> *Master:* Boatswain!
> *Boatswain:* Here, master: what cheer?
> *Mast.:* Good, speak to the mariners: fall to't yarely, or we run ourselves aground: bestir, bestir. (*Exit.*)
> *Enter Mariners.*
> *Boats.:* Heigh, my hearts! cheerly, cheerly, my hearts! yare, yare! Take in the topsail. Tend to the master's whistle.—Blow, till thou burst thy wind, if room enough!

All the roaring, swashing, scrambling, rope-tugging, hard-breathing, of the event are indicated in a few ejaculations. In come passengers; one of them happens to be a king. To his first remark the Boatswain says only: " I pray you now, keep below." " To cabin," " Silence," he proceeds, on interruption from humbler, but still eminent men; and, forced to more remarks, he flings a few arguments over his shoulder, and then roars again: " Cheerly, good hearts! Out of our way I say! "—then rushing off, then returning. He has given a characteristic exhibition of a sailor's attitude to numbskull passengers when there is hard work to be done; in a calm, on the way to Ostend, he would no doubt have leant on a rail and chatted reminiscently to anybody. We see a finely realistic sea-scene, some principals are introduced, we vaguely hear the name of King. Here we are left, at the end of the brief glimpse, on the top of expectation: who are these men, are they to be shipwrecked, are they heroes or villains? The main preliminary exposition is left to the next scene, where there is a conversation, longer than is Shakespeare's wont in such places, between Miranda and Prospero. It is certainly long, but it might be argued that the length is excusable on the ground that it heightens our suspense as to the fate of the distressed ship's company. It also, in the leisurely and detailed manner of its retrospection, differs in character from the normal expository scenes of the mature Shakespeare and reminds us of the closet dramatists. It seems odd from the playwright who said so much and saved so much in Florizel's few natural retrospective words:

> I bless the time
> When my good falcon made her flight across
> Thy father's ground.

But there is a very important fact to note, a fact which enables Shakespeare to pass this scene off. In a general way the objection to this kind of talk may be indicated in phrases such as: "Wouldn't he have told her this before?" or "Why should he tell her now?" or "Could he possibly tell her in this orderly way?" Here we are given, in the very nature of the material, reasons not only for Prospero's present speech but for his previous silence: an exile from humanity, alone with his young daughter, he has never obtruded a detestable past upon her; now, the arrival of people, and such people, on the island, makes communication imperative. Still, one thinks, the scene might have been shorter; but there are many happy touches in it. The opening sentences in it are typical of Shakespeare's true expository method. Miranda in addressing her father—

> If by your art, my dearest father, you have
> Put the wild waters in this roar, allay them.

at once addresses a perfectly natural question and conveys a great deal of information to the audience in so doing: to wit, that her father is a magician, that (for some special reason, no doubt) he has raised the storm which has wrecked the ship which we have just seen, that Miranda herself is a gentle and compassionate girl, and that her relationship with her father is such that she can even plead with him to mitigate the operation of his supernatural powers. Excellent, too, is the gradual adumbration of their past, opening with Prospero's catechism as to what she remembers of her infancy, to which she gropingly replies:

> *Miranda:* 'Tis far off;
> And rather like a dream, than an assurance
> That my remembrance warrants. Had I not
> Four or five women once that tended me?

PLOT, CONSTRUCTION, DEVICE

The precision of this vagueness needs no pointing out—but how well the " four or five " leads us to the revelation of their former status in what is to Miranda " the dark backward and abysm of time."

Though a temptation to bad producers, the opening of *Macbeth* is magnificent, and the subsequent cumulative exposition a model:

> *First Witch:* When shall we three meet again
> In thunder, lightning, or in rain?
> *Second Witch:* When the hurlyburly's done,
> When the battle's lost and won.
> *Third Witch:* That will be ere the set of sun.
> *First Witch:* Where the place?
> *Second Witch:* Upon the heath.
> *Third Witch:* There to meet with Macbeth.
> *First Witch:* I come, Graymalkin!
> *Second Witch:* Paddock calls.
> *Third Witch:* Anon.
> *All:* Fair is foul, and foul is fair:
> Hover through the fog and filthy air. (*Exeunt.*)

Even had those characters not been witches, their dialogue would have set one on the top of expectation.

But the opening of *Hamlet* has never been excelled in drama. It is night on a high platform before the Castle of Elsinore, and the guard is changing. Francisco stands at his post; Bernardo, in the dim light enters to him.

> *Bernardo:* Who's there?
> *Francisco:* Nay, answer me; stand, and unfold yourself.

Bern.: Long live the King!
Fran.: Bernardo?
Bern.: He.
Fran.: You come most carefully upon your hour.
Bern.: 'Tis now struck twelve; get thee to bed, Francisco.
Fran.: For this relief much thanks; 'tis bitter cold,
And I am sick at heart.
Bern.: Have you had quiet guard?
Fran.: Not a mouse stirring.
Bern.: Well, good night.
If you do meet Horatio and Marcellus,
The rivals of my watch, bid them make haste.
Fran.: I think I hear them . . . Stand, ho! Who's there?
(*Enter Horatio and Marcellus.*)

What marvellous dialogue, so realistic, yet so pregnant in its laconicism, so suggestive of things imminent, the bitter cold, the quiet, the underlying sense that something abnormal may well happen, the implication, even, that if it were an ordinary, and not an uncanny night, a " mouse " might have " stirred." Then Francisco's departure, the tense argument about the " dreaded sight " that has already twice been seen, and then Bernardo's words about its appearance last night, " the bell then beating one " (note the word " beating " instead of the dead conventional ' ringing,' ' chiming,' or ' striking '), suddenly interrupted:

PLOT, CONSTRUCTION, DEVICE

Marcellus: Peace! break thee off; look, where it comes again!
(*Enter Ghost.*)
Bernardo: In the same figure, like the king that's dead.
Marcellus: Thou art a scholar; speak to it, Horatio.
Bern.: Looks it not like the king? mark it, Horatio.
Horatio: Most like: it harrows me with fear and wonder.
Bern.: It would be spoke to.
Mar.: Question it, Horatio.
Hor.: What art thou that usurp'st this time of night,
Together with that fair and warlike form
In which the majesty of buried Denmark
Did sometimes march? by heaven I charge thee, speak!
Mar.: It is offended.
Bern.: See! it stalks away.
Hor.: Stay! speak, speak! I charge thee, speak! (*Exit Ghost.*)

Here again curiosity is roused to the highest pitch even whilst we are excited by the happenings before our eyes. Who are these, for whom waits this ghost of Denmark's dead majesty, which will most evidently appear again? When will it speak and what will it say when it does speak? Who sits warm in the lighted halls beyond and below those cold battlements? What peace is there to be broken, what discords await their resolution?

There is an awed discussion about spectres—in the course of which Horatio almost repeats a phrase from *Julius Cæsar*—and then the ghost reappears:

> *Horatio:* I'll cross it, though it blast me.
>   Stay, illusion!
> If thou hast any sound, or use of voice,
> Speak to me:
> If there be any good thing to be done,
> That may to thee do ease and grace to me,
> Speak to me:
> If thou art privy to thy country's fate,
> Which happily foreknowing may avoid,
> O! speak;
> Or if thou hast uphoarded in thy life
> Extorted treasure in the womb of earth,
> For which, they say, you spirits oft walk in
>   death. *(Cock crows.)*
> Speak of it: stay, and speak! Stop it, Marcellus.
>   *Marcellus:* Shall I strike at it with my partisan?
>   *Hor.:* Do, if it will not stand.
>   *Bernardo:*   'Tis here!
>   *Hor.:*   'Tis here! *(Exit Ghost.)*
>   *Mar.:* 'Tis gone!

The mystery is fully unexplained: the fiercer, more desperate, challenge, in that resonant voice, now slowly declamatory, now hurrying and appealing, the repeated silence of the spirit, the vanishing from the fruitless grapples, have intensified expectancy. The passage almost violently supports Mr. Pollard's views about the importance of Shakespeare's punctuation. Before the act is over we know all; we are prepared for the event; that first act has but sharpened our desire to the keenest edge.

What a triumph of stagecraft is *Julius Cæsar*! Listen to Mr. Granville-Barker:

Yet on this monotone the whole gamut of the conspiracy's doubts, fears and desperation is run. Its midway sentence is the steely

" Cassius, be constant "

with which Brutus marks his mastery of the rest. Cæsar is seated. His

" Are we all ready ? "

turns the whole concourse to him. Some few of them are ready indeed. And now in terms of deliberate rhetoric Shakespeare again erects before us the Colossus that is to be overthrown. Then in a flash the blow falls. Butchered by Casca, sacrificed by Brutus—these two doings of the same deed are marked and kept apart—and with no more words about it, Cæsar lies dead.

Remark that we are now only a quarter of the way through the scene; further, that the play's whole action so far has been a preparation for this crisis. Yet, with dead Cæsar lying there, Shakespeare will continue to give us such fresh interest in the living that, with no belittling of the catastrophe, no damping down or desecration of our emotions, our minds will be turned forward still. This is a great technical achievement. He might well have shirked the full attempt and have wound up the scene with its next seventy lines or so. But then could the play ever have recovered strength and impetus? As it is, by the long scene's end our concern for Cæsar is lost in our expectations of the Forum.

Othello, the most nearly perfect in construction of all the tragedies, is as admirable in its expository beginning as elsewhere: the main action begins at once, and before the act ends the note of fatality is firmly struck when Othello is warned that Desdemona may deceive him as she deceived her father. *Lear* plunges almost at once *in medias res*; the brief first conversation but mentions the principal and chiefly bears on the under-plot; a few sentences and Lear himself is on the stage, opening the single and simple action of the play with that unconvincing division of his kingdom and the crude unwarranted outburst against Cordelia:

> How, how, Cordelia! mend your speech a little,
> Lest you may mar your fortunes.

To introduce a central figure so early is seldom done and usually robs a dramatist of a main effect. In *Antony and Cleopatra* the vastness of the theme may have compelled it: ten lines of rapid preparation by Philo is all they get before they sail in, with their eunuchs and their fans. In *Lear* it is a matter of getting rid of one part of the story as soon as possible in order to get as quickly as possible to Lear Agonistes, **the mighty picture of that powerful old**

King's madness and suffering, storms of passion that dominate the storms of nature. There is reason too for the early appearance of Troilus, who is (barring the Prologue, with his " orgulous " and " fraught-age " and " corresponsive and fulfilling bolts " and wanton list of Troy's gates, that is strange Shakespeare, if he wrote it) the first person to speak in the play. Even Lear, for all the personal nature and brief simplicity of his play, was given a perfunctory scene before he stepped on the stage, however hurriedly; though it may be suggested that Lear the King is, dramatically, another character than Lear the discrowned; and, ordinarily, the central character is always prepared for, given a setting and an atmosphere, preluded by his due trumpets or hush of expectation, wrapped in a cloak of romance before he steps from the wings into the light. In *Henry V* it is done by the prologue, which sketches one of those panoramic backgrounds peculiar to Shakespeare. *Macbeth* is preluded by the hags' colloquy in the wilderness, which is there but to set a tone and prepare for a man—not to be spun out into a long witches' Sabbath, by prolonged howlings of wind and swingings to and fro on wires. That Shakespeare did not bother so to prelude and prepare for Troilus shows his consciousness of the fact that Troilus was not the hero of the play, not even as Romeo was, much less as Hamlet or Othello: that his panorama of contending chiefs and armies is not in any sense Troilus's—perhaps could not have been, for in the same measure as we contemn Cressida we must cease to admire (however much we may like) Troilus.

Turn from these stirring and bustling, or awful and premonitory openings, to the first scene of *Twelfth Night*. A room in the Duke's Palace: courtiers and musicians around, the Duke taking his seat, leaning his head on his hand and then ruminatively speaking, asking for a resumption of that strain that has just intoxicated him with its " dying fall ":

Duke: If music be the food of love, play on.

This beginning is like the languid relinquishment of a glove: the mood and atmosphere of the whole untroubled comedy are given at once. It is the most memorable of all the occasions on which Shakespeare, whose sensuousness luxuriated in music, set a tone and indicated an attitude by a call for music —unless we place by it that request of Brutus's to his weary, faithful and beloved child-attendant, when the shadow of to-morrow's death hangs over his sleeplessness and he must have a last touch of sweetness and ease, a last momentary refuge from the tortures of thought and the agonies of responsibility. The opening of *The Merchant of Venice* is a good example of the straight expository opening, natural and progressive, though not especially beautiful or fascinating. That of *King John*, with a fine touch of characterization in its fourth line, introduces us immediately and momentously to the commencing action, whilst informing us as to the reasons for it; the slowness of that of *Henry IV* is justified because of the sense of historical continuity that it gives. Part II of *Henry IV* opens more simply with the help of the admirable prologue—" Rumour, painted full of tongues," who is very humorously characterized while ingeniously giving information illustrative of its own character and necessary to the audience. The beginning of *The Comedy of Errors*, intolerably laborious, and slow, cannot be defended at all—though it may very well be explained away as not Shakespeare's. It is comic that the last line of this weary and languid first scene should be

But to procrastinate his lifeless end.

Shakespeare did not perpetrate such openings unless in simultaneous collaboration.

Even in successive collaboration he would have amended it. At however early an age, it must have made him impatient, though he passed some dilatory and lifeless passages later. One way or another, usually very rapidly and naturally, he gets the work of exposition done and sets his atmosphere, with that economy which he also exhibits in so many scene and subscene beginnings. How effective is the " Sister Anne, sister Anne " opening to *Othello*, Act II, in spite of the rumbustious speeches in it! How deliciously rousing Sly's first waking words; " For God's sake, a pot of small ale! "—natural, yet unexpected, greatly enriched by the circumstances in which they are spoken, provocative of instant curiosity as to what they will lead to—a parallel to many such a predicament befalling the porters, barbers and calendars of the *Arabian Nights*. *Coriolanus*, I. 5, following immediately on the battle of doubtful issue, opens with certain Romans carrying spoils in a street:

> *First Roman:* This will I carry to Rome.
> *Second Roman:* And I this.
> *Third Roman:* A murrain on't! I took this for silver.

That is all they say: not a word more. Yet in those few words they convey the upshot thus far of the first fight, the nature of their pillage, their state of mind, and the contrast with their general, who at once steps in and denounces them as pilferers and almost deserters. Equally packed is Demetrius's sentence in the first scene of *Antony and Cleopatra* after the pair, in all their oriental splendour, have passed across the stage:

> I am full sorry
> That he approves the common liar, who
> Thus speaks of him at Rome

—a sentence surely preluding the strife of East and West, wonderfully conjuring up the panorama of a world's gossip, indicating the double view of Antony's faults, seen through friendly and through unfriendly eyes, indicating also the main charge against him (that he wasted his time in dalliance), the alleged motive of his enemies and the real reason of his inevitable downfall. Wonderfully in *Julius Cæsar* he conjures up a crowd in the lines:

" Hence! home, you idle creatures, get you home. Is this a holiday ? " But that gift of suggesting an outside world and its atmosphere is perhaps most triumphantly shown in the early scenes of *Troilus and Cressida*, which is primarily a panoramic play. At greater length we get it in Hubert's speech about the English population at a moment of crisis:

> Old men and beldams in the streets
> Do prophesy upon it dangerously:
> Young Arthur's death is common in their mouths;
> And when they talk of him, they shake their heads
> And whisper one another in the ear;
> And he that speaks doth gripe the hearer's wrist,
> Whilst he that hears makes fearful action,
> With wrinkled brows, with nods, with rolling eyes.
> I saw a smith stand with his hammer, thus,
> The whilst his iron did on the anvil cool,
> With open mouth swallowing a tailor's news;
> Who, with his shears and measure in his hand,
> Standing on slippers,—which his nimble haste
> Had falsely thrust upon contrary feet,—
> Told of a many thousand warlike French,
> That were embattailed and rank'd in Kent.
> Another lean unwash'd artificer
> Cuts off his tale and talks of Arthur's death.

That passage also (if the digression be permitted) is notable for several other reasons. It is one of the very few passages (*The Merry Wives* is a whole play in such a setting) in Shakespeare which have the sort of 'small country town' atmosphere with which he must have been familiar at Stratford. It illustrates that amazing narrative gift which was but maturing when he wrote his two long poems. Its brief strong characterization, its grouping and movement and strong visualization of things physical related to things psychical show the qualities which made him inevitably a dramatist. His astonishing clarity and compactness of language are shown; also that fertility of conception which led him sometimes to superfluity—he could not help seeing the hurried tailor pulling the left shoe on the right foot, and, having seen it, he had to mention it, though it had very little place in a play in which the tailor did not elsewhere appear. These qualities appear in a hundred descriptions of events offstage, descriptions usually dull in the theatre but in Shakespeare vivid to the point of television. We may recall Act II, Scene 3, of *Richard II*—it must never be forgotten that " Scene 3, the Wolds in Gloucestershire," comes, if quite sensibly, from editors and not from our author, so negligent of print, so sure of indicating producer's treatment through his text:

> *Boling.:* How far is it, my lord, to Berkeley now?
> *North.:* Believe me, noble lord,
> I am a stranger here in Gloucestershire:
> These high wild hills and rough uneven ways
> Draw out our miles and make them wearisome.

Shakespeare was next door to being a " Cotsall man," took a pride in the Cotswold bareness and its strangeness to strangers, and in a few lines rendered unnecessary all the ' scenery ' that he lacked and that the modern theatre (though we are returning to plainness and the appeal to the imagination) possesses. We may recall, also, Buckingham's account to Richard III of his interview with the mayor and citizens who stood " like dumb statues," which makes also a thrilling dramatic transition. Such passages, dramatically powerful, range in length from that to the servant's:

> I heard him say Brutus and Cassius
> Are rid like madmen through the gates of Rome.

The stage set and the play begun—the audience, in fact, being precisely informed *what the play is about*—Shakespeare's " conduct of the fable," as Johnson remarked, is usually excellent. Though there be perhaps no play technically perfect (which scholarship may in the long run decide to be due to the intractability of his second-hand material or his own impatience about taking the last pains with revision), there is no play which has not signal technical moments which show his mastery of stage story-telling. The movement, once begun, is sustained, the tempo increases at the due places, and all concatenates to a satisfactory end. Movement between scenes is skilfully indicated, and the interlude scenes (even such as Bottom's acting) give one the sense of 'getting on.' Movement proceeds equably, or hustles: it is seldom arrested.

The characters, who are, as a rule, nicely balanced and well proportioned in their prominence, are, as characters, discussed elsewhere. The character, once presented, rarely acts 'out of character.' Shakespeare is careful about motivation—except occasionally with his first assumptions (assumptions which presumably did not harass his contemporaries as they do us): Portia's assent to the casket, Antonio's bond, Posthumus' bet, Lear's division—usually making his characters act so naturally that the plot in detail appears to spring inevitably from them, rather than they to be fitted into it. Here we may notice the skill with which Shakespeare introduces and displays them, brings them in and takes them off, in the interests of his moving fable. A small scene is saved by the first description we have of Romeo, before he appears on the stage. A person and a condition are made rapidly known to us, as (though less necessarily and purely for the delight of presentation) when Barnardine in prison is described:

> *Provost:* A man that apprehends death no more dreadfully but as a drunken sleep; careless, reckless, and fearless of what's past, present, or to come; insensible of mortality, and desperately mortal.
> *Duke:* He wants advice.
> *Provost:* He will hear none. He hath evermore had the liberty of the prison: give him

leave to escape hence, he would not: drunk many times a day, if not many days entirely drunk. We have very oft awaked him, as if to carry him to execution, and showed him a seeming warrant for it: it hath not moved him at all.

It is as vivid and indicative as Hortensio's account of Catherine's rage or Norfolk's description of Wolsey:

> *Norfolk:* My lord, we have
> Stood here observing him; some strange commotion
> Is in his brain: he bites his lip and starts;
> Stops on a sudden, looks upon the ground,
> Then lays his finger on his temple; straight
> Springs out into fast gait; then stops again,
> Strikes his breast hard; and anon he casts
> His eye against the moon: in most strange postures
> We have seen him set himself.
> *King Henry:* It may well be:
> There is a mutiny in's mind.

There is character in action off-stage. It may be noted here that Wolsey, later, dies off-stage: and that his death ' off ' adds, as does this present indirection, to his mysterious and pathetic magnitude.

Even more briefly is the colour of a mind shown in Cæsar's description of Cassius:

> Such men as he be never at heart's ease
> Whiles they behold a greater than themselves.

Off-stage indication again is present in *The Merchant of Venice*:

> *Portia:* Ay, that's a colt indeed, for he doth nothing but talk of his horse; and he makes it a great appropriation to his own good parts that he can shoe him himself. I am much afeard my lady his mother played false with a smith.
> *Nerissa:* Then is there the County Palatine.
> *Portia:* He doth nothing but frown, as who should say, 'An you will not have me, choose.' He hears merry tales, and smiles not; I fear he will prove the weeping philosopher when he grows old, being so full of unmannerly sadness in his youth.

What excitement, again, is roused by Lucius' description to Brutus of the conspirators who have come to the door:

> *Brutus:* Do you know them?
> *Lucius:* No, sir; their hats are pluck'd about their ears
> And half their faces buried in their cloaks.

While in the same play Shakespeare keeps Antony wonderfully up his sleeve, letting him scarcely speak until his great scene, but having him constantly alluded to and described.

This gift of summary description he employs to great purpose in indicating characters just before they come on the stage—as Sir Andrew in *Twelfth Night*:

PLOT, CONSTRUCTION, DEVICE

> *Maria:* That quaffing and drinking will undo you: I heard my lady talk of it yesterday; and of a foolish knight that you brought in one night here to be her wooer.
> *Sir T.:* Who? Sir Andrew Aguecheek?
> *Maria:* Ay, he.
> *Sir T.:* He's as tall a man as any's in Illyria.
> *Maria:* What's that to the purpose?
> *Sir T.:* Why, he has three thousand ducats a year.
> *Maria:* Ay, but he'll have but a year in all these ducats: he's a very fool and a prodigal.
> *Sir T.:* Fie, that you'll say so! he plays o' the viol-de-gamboys, and speaks three or four languages word for word without book, and hath all the good gifts of nature.
> *Maria:* He hath indeed, almost natural; for, besides that he's a fool, he's a great quarreller; and but that he hath the gift of a coward to allay the gust that he hath in quarrelling, 'tis thought among the prudent he would quickly have the gift of a grave.

The whole complexion of the man is succinctly waved across the footlights: then he comes in, and the fun begins. Thus is the entry of Benedick prepared for in the very words which serve to characterize Beatrice herself by her view of him and her way of expressing it, and also the previous stations of the two:

> *Leonato:* What is he that you asked for, niece?
> *Hero:* My cousin means Signior Benedick of Padua.

> *Messenger:* O! he is returned, and as pleasant as ever he was.
>
> *Beatrice:* He set up his bills here in Messina and challenged Cupid at the flight; and my uncle's fool, reading the challenge, subscribed for Cupid, and challenged him at the bird-bolt. I pray you, how many hath he killed and eaten in these wars? But how many hath he killed? for, indeed, I promised to eat all of his killing.

Less specific, but equally effective in its way (as also, we discover, in its indication of Bassanio's inadequacy to the appreciation of the entire Portia) is the first mention of Portia, shortly to enter.

> In Belmont is a lady richly left,
> And she is fair, and fairer than that word.

Entries prepared, the principals appear and disclose themselves with superb rapidity. Hamlet's first speech is an aside, his second a cry: the entry is wonderfully revelatory and dramatic. After we have heard a few exchanges between Beatrice and Benedick, we feel as though we knew their past for ten years back; and what could be swifter and surer than Shylock's first introduction:

> *Shylock:* Three thousand ducats; well?
> *Bassanio:* Ay, sir, for three months.
> *Shy.:* For three months; well?
> *Bass.:* For the which, as I told you, Antonio shall be bound.
> *Shy.:* Antonio shall become bound; well?

PLOT, CONSTRUCTION, DEVICE 111

Within thirty lines the man's character, the status of his race, his and their relations with their Gentile neighbours, are all most laconically set out. With such swift indications of relation the plays bristle. No better or more compact example could be quoted than that which is given when Henry VIII and Suffolk step out into the gallery from the private room:

> *King Henry:* Charles, I will play no more to-night;
> My mind's not on't; you are too hard for me.
> *Suffolk:* Sir, I did never win of you before.
> *King Henry:* But little, Charles;
> Nor shall not when my fancy's on my play.

(And there are, one may remark parenthetically, people who suppose that Shakespeare had never frequented what is called ' good society.')

Nothing could be more economical than his methods of introducing and displaying his characters: having shown them, he lets them act, except when the fore-ordained plots thwart them, as they would act; and quickly. His characters as a rule go off as naturally as they enter. A fine instance of his power of moving them occurs in *Coriolanus*, where the whole stage of jabbering servants is cleared in a moment with " In, in, in, in ! " as it is realized that the diners within have risen. Another exit, very effective because in other hands or in another context it would be ineffective, is Ely's in *Richard III*, III. 4. He is sent off to get strawberries: a transparent excuse, no doubt, but as it comes, it comes, and perfectly naturally, from the subtle, dictatorial Richard—not from Shakespeare. He does not often leave us with the impression that it is he who is shifting his characters on and off: they are moving of their own volition or under the sway of stronger wills or powers than their own.

Yet " holding the mirror up to nature " is not all. No man ever made a good play by exhibiting what is called ' a slice of life '—which usually means a very small and desiccated slice with all the plums omitted. Even when characters ' as large as life,' and a thrilling story, have been outlined, there is still stage presentation to be considered, which involves stage device. Shakespeare's great forte was the art which conceals art, the plan which seems natural, the intrusion and operation which appear inevitable.

And in detail he disdained none of the theatrical tricks which add salt, in the theatre, to particular scenes, apart from the impression of life given by the general talk and dialogue. The tricks of the trade were not numerous when he began writing; they were much more numerous when he finished. No dramatist of that age so cunningly played with the audience by references to it in the play. The *Hamlet* passage must have silenced the " barren spectators " awhile; in *Henry V* the audience is appealed to to help out the author; the most daringly imaginative stroke of the kind occurs in *Julius Cæsar*, where a double dye of reality and

PLOT, CONSTRUCTION, DEVICE

romance is given to the murder by Cassius' exclamation:

> How many ages hence
> Shall this our lofty scene be acted o'er,
> In states unborn and accents yet unknown!

and Brutus' reply:

> How many times shall Cæsar bleed in sport,
> That now on Pompey's basis lies along
> No worthier than the dust!

None has equalled his fertility and certainty with suspense, turns and twists that prelude the inevitable, hesitations and ambiguities which hold an audience on tenterhooks, even though rationally it knows what must happen. *Macbeth* is one long suspense. Surprise he habitually used, whether the surprise of sudden action or that of sudden disclosure, the unexpected swiftness of Cæsar's death, Cleopatra's maniacal spring upon the messenger, her rush to buckle Antony's armour when his servant fumbles, an action that clutches at the throat; sudden revelation by disguised people or the surprise of intervention from without, the Duke's deceit in *Measure for Measure*, or the noise like a fray, that the wind blows from the Capitol to Brutus' Portia. He had a marvellous gift of tersely describing backgrounds: in a sentence he will sometimes indicate what would afford a modern dramatist half a page of stage directions—a few properties there were on his stage, but no scenery to speak of: with a sentence he could indicate a world around better than it could be indicated by all the machinery, scenery and lighting of the modern stage. In his largest manner is the indication of a vast panorama during the Greek debate in *Troilus*. By the same token, he was acutely aware of the importance of background, and exploited what is called the 'pathetic fallacy,' though he never knew its name, making earth groan with the groans of men, and preparing a background of eclipse for the sombre revolutions of the human mind and the obscure sufferings of the human soul. Think of the general settings of any of the plays, then ask: 'Where else could it happen?' Storms and sunlight, brooks and trees, banqueting halls and shepherds' huts—they are all chosen with exquisite appropriateness. Seasons, hours, revolutions of day and night are cunningly used also. 'Deeds of darkness' are done in darkness: night scenes were almost a hobby with him. "He bestows upon his play," Professor Matthews says of *Othello*, "all the picturesque accessories of which the plot was capable. He gives us torches by night, a solemn sitting of the stately council, a riot suddenly raised under the silent stars, and the loud clangour of the island bells."

There are flitting ghosts in his shadowy night-landscapes, and sleep-walkers, and the moans of uneasy sleepers. He knew also the effect of clocks, in producing verisimilitude, and also in emphasizing the unnatural hours, if the unnatural hours were in question. All clocks strike the same note: 'Remember!' He knew it, and the intervention of clocks and the hour was such a habit with him that one is tempted to think that he had been profoundly impressed by that prodigious clock-scene in Marlowe where Faustus agonizes at the remorseless progress of the dial hand that draws him towards his doom. In the theatre, silence and the beat of a clock's bell will always make our hearts stand still; a watchman calling the hour will always give us the feeling of expectancy which preludes strange or momentous events. "It's one o'clock, boy, is't not?" says Gardiner, as the fifth act of *Henry VIII* opens. "It hath struck," replies the boy. The passage of time is with us, in *Julius Cæsar*, II. 1, from Brutus's first observation of the stars, to his order that the boy should go to bed (while " the exhalations whizzing in the air " give the master light to read by): to the first break of dawn in " yon grey lines "; to the striking of three by the clock (" Peace, count the clock! "); to the appearance in the orchard of Portia, committing herself to " the raw cold morning "—and the clock is at the kernel of it all.

That scene in *Cymbeline* in which Iachimo plays his foul nocturnal trick is thus preluded:

> *Imogen:* What hour is it?
> *Lady:*   Almost midnight, madam.
> *Imo.:* I have read three hours then; mine
>   eyes are weak;
> Fold down the leaf where I have left; to bed:
> Take not away the taper, leave it burning,

> And if thou canst awake by four o' the clock,
> I prithee, call me. Sleep hath seized me wholly.

The hour; the book closed at the end of a chapter; the taper that consumes while men sleep—they are also used, naturally yet as momentous emblems, in *Julius Cæsar*.

The second act of *Macbeth* opens with the clean emphasis of the hour. Banquo enters, the boy with the torch before him:

> *Banquo:* How goes the night, boy?
> *Fleance:* The moon is down; I have not heard the clock.
> *Ban.:* And she goes down at twelve.
> *Fle.:* I take't, 'tis later, sir.

Essentially, to the 'fable' it matters not; but " the noon of night " has an effect on us, so it is used, as the still more abnormal hour of one mentioned (at past twelve) in the first scene of *Hamlet*. The certainty with which Shakespeare uses the hour of day to suggest the atmosphere he wants is characteristic of him.

There are some who think that even his language was cunningly adapted to produce 'atmosphere.' 'World,' we are told, is the typical word of *Antony and Cleopatra*. Here I doubt the deliberation: the desired atmosphere being what it was, Shakespeare could not help producing the words.

In trick, device and fantasy, large and small, Shakespeare was inexhaustible. He ranged from the Roman severity of *Coriolanus* to the Arcadian opulence of the *Dream*, able, on the one hand, to write a strict play in which all should be subordinated to the realistic play of human passions in an all too real world, and, on the other, to create forms " more real than living man " of fairies and monsters, embracing the imaginations of the French naturalists, of Dickens and Smollett, and of Hans Andersen, and freely projecting all upon the stage. His age delighted in a show: he gave it dances, music and flittings of supernatural beings, aiming often at pleasing by a diversity of spectacle rather than by a rigid and coherent development of theme. Occasionally he even assented to the masque and pageant element—always an interruption—so popular in those days. But a student of the masque passages in *Henry VIII*, in *Cymbeline* and *The Tempest* may well conclude none of them to be his, and argue from this that he did often surrender to the suspension of action by a ' revue number,' however splendid and sonorous.

Mr. Granville-Barker says:

The Elizabethan drama made an amazingly quick advance from crudity to an excellence which was often technically most elaborate. The advance and the not less amazing gulf which divides its best from its worst may be ascribed to the simplicity of the machinery it employed. That its decadence was precipitated by the influence of the Mask and the shifting of its centre of interest from the barer public stage to the candle-lit private theatre, where the machinery of the Mask became effective, it would be rash to assert; but the occurrences are suspiciously related. Man and machine (here at least is a postulate, if a platitude!) are false allies in the theatre, secretly at odds; and when man gets the worst of it, drama is impoverished; and the struggle, we may add, is eternal.

Shakespeare knew this well enough. I doubt if he wrote a masque.

In developing his themes themselves he had a remarkable eye for stage effect, not shrinking from the most palpable thrills of melodrama and anticipating the subtlest 'stunts' of the modern stage. "What ho, Pisanio!" cried out three times by Imogen in the very midst of her protests to Iachimo, who seems a seducer: it is so effective on the stage that we forget all about the improbability of the story! The procession of ghosts in *Richard III* (though it might have been more effective had Richard alone and not Richmond been addressed) is a melodramatic device of the first water: the antiphonal dialogue of the mourning Queens, dark, statuesque, subdued, in the same play makes us think of the monochrome effects of Maeterlinck. His use of contrast, of the sudden irruption, of the calm before, and the calm after, the storm is a matter of commonplace. The knock and chatter of the porter in *Macbeth* (intrinsically so feeble that one can hardly believe it to be by him, or at least must suppose he rapidly interpolated it during rehearsals) is the most celebrated instance: the light of every day invades an infernal and bloodshot darkness. Of his premonitory hushes (hushes comparatively) there is none better than the scene in *Henry V* before Agincourt—that quiet compressed conversation (there is a whole novel in it) of soldiers possibly doomed to die on the morrow.

An inventor of large effects, he was also a master of the minor mechanics of plot. Antony's use of Cæsar's mantle, so concrete a thing, so full of associations, is perhaps on a higher plane than most things which one has classed as dramatic tricks: but it needed invention. Handkerchief clues, symmetrical pairs of lovers, concocted letters and disguised girls to-day seem lower than most. That is because we have had too much of them. In his day they were new and must have been striking. Such as they were, he exploited them thoroughly: Viola's disguise, and her carrying of a message from the man she loved to another woman, was but Julia's performance in *The Two Gentlemen* repeated: and her confusing resemblance to Sebastian had been anticipated in *The Comedy of Errors*, The comic lesson in *The Taming of the Shrew*, III. 1, forecasts the comedy of Beaumarchais and Sheridan; no man has ever excelled the trick in *Henry IV*, Part I, where first the Prince and then Falstaff assume majesty and discuss their relations. What an admirable stratagem it is in *Lear* when Edgar leads Gloucester to the top of the imagined cliff, all the dizzying suggestions of height are described and believed, and the despairing but deluded Duke goes through the sensations of falling to find himself prone and intact on the ground: the palm of suicide without the dust.

One of his favourite stage devices was the exhibition of somebody acting in the presence of watchers to him invisible. Malvolio is the supreme example, soliloquizing to the winds and birds, in imagination on a footing with the loftiest spirits of creation and smiled on by nature's paragon, in fact will-o'-the-wisped and bewrayed by two bibulous knights and a pair of scandalous servants, who make for the audience a running commentary as he talks. Parolles is similarly overheard; so also the pathetic Wolsey; so Othello hears and annotates the devil's playing of Cassio—a scene (*Othello*, IV. 1) astutely handled, but to me rather below the dignity of the play and the hero of it. From Malvolio to Macbeth the stratagem is used—with the utmost pith and dramatic subtlety when Ulysses and the tortured Troilus, with Thersites jeering in their wake, observe and currently comment on Diomedes' love-making with Cressida, every 'reaction' of every faithless sentence being briefly made. The one play in which, perhaps, he overdoes the hiding and listening is *Hamlet*, where Polonius (though he is merely hiding and not speaking) is killed at the second attempt. No more than an indication of his 'dodges' for stage effect can be given here: think but of Edgar's sudden resort to rustic dialect for a disguise, and of Lucius talking in his sleep:

PLOT, CONSTRUCTION, DEVICE

Brutus: Didst thou dream, Lucius, that thou so criedst out?
Lucius: My lord, I do not know that I did cry.
Bru.: Yes, that thou didst. Didst thou see any thing?
Luc.: Nothing, my lord.
Bru.: Sleep again, Lucius.

It seems so natural, we are so familiar with it, that we tend to forget that it is art, and that anything else might have been made to happen.

That comes at the end of the fourth act; the fifth act is to complete the tragedy. This is the hush before catastrophe, the heavy and boding air of night about to discharge its lightnings, the strain of the soul near breaking-point. Of all those pregnant nights in Shakespeare, nights of dark, timorous or lovely deeds, these are among the most memorable, the nights before irrevocable crime or irrevocable doom. In *Julius Cæsar* there are two such; the night before Philippi is the consequence and the parallel of the night before the murder of Cæsar. In both is a great event prepared by whispers amid the darkness that awaits the inevitable and relentless dawn, which brings once the prepared and deliberate slaying, and once its retribution. Brutus and the boy are in both. But at Philippi the boy, symbolically, has grown tired, and Brutus, still resolute in his narrow nobility, is as one who has grown too tired to sleep, and has nothing left in life but to await the last fight and die well. He has shed his autumnal foliage and his tree stands with bare and writhen limbs against the stars. As momentous is the burdened night before Bosworth: Richard seeking his tent and troubled bed after the last preparations have been perfected, and the last footsteps have died away, nothing now remaining but the morrow's issue, which we await with him as though to us also it were heavy with impending doom. In the comic plays it is a tangled knot that awaits rapid resolution, by a dramatist's skill; in the tragedies an atmosphere, a situation which must of its own nature break, a mighty arching wave, curved to its thinnest crest and an instant at rest before it topples in reverberating ruin. The hand of Shakespeare was, when he willed, unerring in preparation for catastrophe, and his finest endings are unparalleled in literature.

There is the ending of comedy and the ending of tragedy, the ending of the theatre and the ending of life, the ending of a day and the ending of all our days. It is comedy: ultimates shall be forgotten; risks have been run and fortunately run, misunderstandings have been engendered and dispelled; plots have been hatched against virtue and the angels have foiled them; circumstances have conspired against vice and on behalf of virtue: at the last moment all has gone well. None has more effectively (and, on occasion, more impudently, so as to secure a perfectly Arcadian contour) left his lovers in each other's arms than Shakespeare restored his princes to their thrones—rebellion withered, the sun shining, the larks singing. **He** could show his persons, as he could himself be, and as we can be, content in the felicity of an hour. "As you like it" and "What you will": life seems long and we like 'a happy ending.' But it is no ending.

For the deeper and the more personal note sounds at the end of the tragedies. "Unto this end come one and all"—

> We are such stuff
> As dreams are made on, and our little life
> Is rounded with a sleep.

This was Shakespeare's dominant thought: why call it an obsession, since it springs from the very centre and core of our knowledge and experience? Gay as he was, prone to jollity, determined to "lie i' the sun" and be grateful to the sun, rejoicing as he did in the richness of life, responsive as he was to all its warmth, colour and variety, he was a man perpetually aware of death, knowing that "to this favour must we all come." That preoccupation is constantly disclosed in his verse, and is expressed with an iron firmness in the endings of many of his plays.

There was, said Maurice Hewlett, something icy under all his passion: and from this the frigidity came. Maurice Hewlett and God bless the soul of that chivalrous man—objected; but Maurice Hewlett is dead and under the Wiltshire clay. Later, as Shakespeare would have reflected, he may serve to stop a bung-hole. Shakespeare was preoccupied with what our own time has learned to call " the riddle of the Universe." Some of the terms have changed. We are no longer Ptolemaic, but in essence the riddle remains what it was.

Life has existed on this planet for millions of years, human life for hundreds of thousands. The earth was a ball of fire, then a swamp in which life germinated from amœba to brontosaurus. Then through æons, while the polar ice crept forward and back, the ascending scale climbed towards man. Grunts evolved with us to speech; the first flint was carved, the first corn planted, the first boat launched, the first hut built. After unimaginable years empires were founded which perished in the sands thousands of years ago, leaving few traces or none. Came Egypt, came Assyria, came Greece, came Rome (while the millions in China, India, Peru, swarmed and died in the distance); came Christianity, and then all those crowded short years recorded in our histories. Then ourselves were born.

We are, we think when we are not thinking, at the apex of time: our lives seem long compared with all those myriad generations before us. However far we may have crept towards our earthly goal, death is still a thing we feel we can postpone indefinitely: any other may be struck down to-morrow, but not ourselves. We act accordingly: strut, scheme, lie awake at nights worrying, intrigue for our children, advertise for ourselves, lay deep trains which shall bring us at last to some barn full of Dead Sea fruit. Yet, given a minute of solitary meditation, we see it all in the eternal perspective. So brief are we in the long history of the earth. So brief is the earth's history in the history of the Universe. Before ever life began on this planet, it may have waxed and waned, not perhaps in our forms, but culminating in a self-consciousness like ours, in other planets of our system. And before our system was, before our sun was, elsewhere in space, that story may have been told, and told innumerable times. They were born, and died, and their world after them, in the unimaginable deeps of time: creatures of whatever shape, who learned at last to plan, to love, to meditate on divinity, to stand in awe under other stars than ours; for there are elder and younger, sons of the morning and patriarchs, even in the august company of the constellations; and time may have been when none that we know were anywhere visible, yet clear eyes looked at stars spread like a bright veil on the fathomless face of night. A generation—and eternity! Mayflies, ephemerides, atomies of a moment: that is what we are, and these very lines as they are now written, though they live for a hundred years, are, in the light of astronomic time, as though they had never been written, like the season's leaves that fell from the poplars in Paradise, or the scales that were shed by the fish that lived in the moon's sea, now immemorially dry. The mind reels at the contemplation of time, and time, and time, backward and forward—not only because it is not to be grasped, but also because it means death, and death, and death. In the enchantment of metaphysic we may at moments transcend it all: we need not bother about understanding; our " immortal longings " have an eternal root and will have an eternal satisfaction; time is but an illusion; present, past and future signify nothing. Yet in time we love and in time we suffer, and in time as our friends have died, so shall we die also. At a month the child may first follow its mother with its eyes, at two months it may first voluntarily smile; after certain other months it may clasp and coo at a shining spoon, crawl, sit upright, walk, talk. Yet so also did the children in Memphis, Tyre, and Ur of the Chaldees. The first age leads to the seventh, and the seventh is on the verge of death: the child, the boy, the young man, the man, the middle-aged man, the aging man, the agèd man, come in remorseless sequence, and then there is the step over the threshold, taken never so unwillingly unto:

> the bourn from which no traveller returns.

With this thought Shakespeare was daily familiar: he had an incubus and it chanted ' *Souviens-toi.*' The beginnings of his tragedies might have been the ' ends ' of comedies: what better end for a comedy than the triumph of Coriolanus, or (better still) the marriage of Othello, after many wars and a long struggle with his comrades, to the loveliest daughter of Venice ? But the ends of his comedies were

PLOT, CONSTRUCTION, DEVICE 127

more surely the beginnings of tragedies, of one tragedy. Reconciled Bertram might be to Helena —but which of them would die first, and how would the other die? Married Portia might be to Bassanio, yet death has no truck with ducats. All the badinage of Beatrice and Benedick may have dwindled into sweet murmurs in a bed: yet ' a little while ' and where were they? If they came from an Italian novel—dead long since, and in pain, and one surviving the other. If they were Shakespeare's contemporaries—dead a little before him, or a little after him, their bodies in decay, their spirits quenched or gone in quest of that which living man can but guess and vaguely represent by the images of living man drawn from the chronicles of a single ball of earth. In the tragedies the curtain really falls. By one road or another the end of all men is reached, and the wisest, most charitable, most eloquent of spectators sings the Requiem, paying his tribute to genius, courage and virtue, before he too descends into that hole in the ground which received the slow steps of Everyman. And that spectator is ready with an epitaph, so that an epitaph be earned:

> He was a man. Take him for all in all
> We shall not look upon his like again

and:

> For he was great of heart

and:

> For he was likely, had he been put on,
> To have proved most royally

and:
> O! let him pass; he hates him
> That would upon the rack of this tough world
> Stretch him out longer

and:

> Now boast thee, death, in thy possession lies
> A lass unparallel'd.

Yet the royalty would have passed, and the prolonged pains of the rack: what the poets called mutability was to Shakespeare no conventional elegiac theme, but the abiding background of all his thought. Mutability, mortality—they are the same thing: and it gave him those magnificent closes, stormy or sad, culminating in the long adagio of Cleopatra's end, the last action of which is prepared for as royally and elaborately as she prepared herself for it, taking crown and robe and vesting herself royally. Before the fourth act is over, when Antony moans his last passionate music, the end has been begun, and, under all the fluctuations of surface events, its progress is audible. The sad melody breaks out clear and loud with Iras's exclamation:

> Finish, good lady; the bright day is done
> And we are for the dark.

There are brief interruptions that serve to quicken the Queen's intention to kill herself, and then with one last imperial speech she parts from her women and the world which "is not worth leave-taking." With a sad jest she puts the serpent to her breast.

Iras lies senseless at her feet. Charmian in exquisite despair cries: " O eastern star! "

> *Cleopatra*: Peace, peace!
> Dost thou not see my baby at my breast
> That sucks the nurse asleep?
> *Charmian:* O, break! O, break!
> *Cleo.:* As sweet as balm, as soft as air, as gentle—
> O Antony!—Nay, I will take thee too.
> (*Applying another asp to her arm.*)
> What should I stay— (*Dies.*)

It was the kiss of the asp of death that was " of many thousand kisses the poor last." The great protagonists have gone. Octavius comes on, as Lodovico and Fortinbras elsewhere, a hasty epilogue, the invasion of common light, the token of continuity and the indifference of nature. " We have seen the best of our time. There is nothing left remarkable." We are left with that feeling, profoundly planted, even at the end of *Richard III* when we have had our last glimpse of him, horseless, fearless in his ferocity, ready still to " stand the hazard of the die " after a day's carnage, rushing off again to fall at once: a superb ending, almost enlisting our sympathies for " the bloody dog ": villainy is quenched, but so is glorious vitality; the dramatist has triumphantly done his work.

The end of *Lear*—a play which might be described as almost all ending and very little beginning—is astounding in its sequence of emotions expressed in almost superhuman dialogue. No sooner has the old man begun his career of dignified old age with a hundred knights in retinue, than his daughters begin reducing his train and disregarding all his wishes. Thenceforward it is linkèd bitterness long drawn out. He storms and raves, he tries to take action; then, frustrated, he goes mad and renounces the whole order of life; then the tension becomes too much: he breaks, and is a poor old man, self-reproachful and meekly ready for anything that a half-realized world may inflict upon him. Every trick of the dramatist's cunning and every stop of the poet's organ is employed in this masterly progression. The distraction of the discrowned monarch is emphasized by the poor trimmings he pulls from the hedgerows: Lear in his madness is crowned with weeds as Ophelia with flowers; one, broken, lapses into the lunacy of wild despair, the other into the lunacy of awful gaiety. His tempest blows itself out. When "the great rage is kill'd in him," his powers are exhausted: he cannot even rouse himself to a faith in the returned Cordelia—if she too wishes to beat him, his head is ready bowed for the deserved blow; he is like an old outcast dog gone half-blind. "You do me wrong to take me out o' the grave," is the most he can say in self-defence; and then, when she persists:

>   Pray, do not mock me:
> I am a very foolish fond old man,
> Fourscore and upward, not an hour more or less;
> And, to deal plainly,
> I fear I am not in my perfect mind.

He is almost past suffering: it was an excess of cruelty, though dramatically magnificent, on Shakespeare's part, to give him once more a glimpse of humble happiness.

> *Lear:* Come, let's away to prison;
> We two alone will sing like birds i' the cage:
> When thou dost ask me blessing, I'll kneel down,
> And ask of thee forgiveness: so we'll live,
> And pray, and sing, and tell old tales, and laugh
> At gilded butterflies, and hear poor rogues
> Talk of court news.

For then came the cruellest stroke of all, and a return of the old violence, which is followed by a deeper subsidence than ever, and the hopelessness now, not of derangement, but of *sanity*. Lear dies sane " upon the rack of this tough world," sane and not petrified. And all Shakespeare's powers, of visualization, of entering into the feelings of human beings under great stress, of expressing these and the colour of character in vital images and brief sentences wrung straight from the heart, whilst reinforcing the sorrow of his fable with the cadence of his syllables, are employed on that last sub-scene. " I know when one is dead, and when one lives," says the old man, simple in his grief, not ratiocinating as to whether everyone does not share that elementary knowledge:

> Lend me a looking-glass;
> If that her breath will mist or stain the stone,
> Why, then she lives.

He holds a feather before her lips. He thinks it stirs. The others murmur compassionately. He knows she is dead. He recalls the accents he will never hear again, the virile, positive view of him coming out in his very commendation:

> Her voice was ever soft,
> Gentle and low, an excellent thing in woman.

The warrior in him flares up as he remembers that he killed her murderer. The officer, kindly humouring, confirms him:

> Did I not, fellow?
> I have seen the day, with my good biting
>   falchion
> I would have made them skip: I am old now,
> And these same crosses spoil me. Who are you?
> Mine eyes are not o' the best.

He hears news, diverse and tragic. "Ay, so I think," he mumbles, and: "You are welcome hither." Then the full force of his desolation breaks over him, and he dies in an agony of dreadful illumination:

> And my poor fool is hang'd! No, no, no life!
> Why should a dog, a horse, a rat, have life,
> And thou no breath at all? Thou'lt come no
>   more,
> Never, never, never, never, never!
> Pray you, undo this button: thank you, sir.
> Do you see this? Look on her, look, her lips,
> Look there, look there!

It is the anguish of our whole race typified!

The whole play has that air: it is terror, darkness and suffering unmitigated. It is characteristic of it that here alone (for the revolting pie, the severed hands, the basket, etc., of *Titus* cannot be reckoned) do we find anything as monstrous as the plucking out of Gloucester's eyes on the stage and the trampling of one of them underfoot—not to be lightly dismissed as a pandering to the " sadist tastes of the time " (which Shakespeare showed no general inclination to gratify and was, as I think, temperamentally bound to loathe and despise), but surely coming out of a resolve (however misguided) to look the extremes of human degradation and brutality in the face. Such things have been: it may be salutary to confront them. " Things are what they are, their consequences will be what they will be; why then should we deceive ourselves ? "

Lear is a tortured Prometheus, with lost affections to make him more wretched, with no hope to fortify him, with no self-sacrifice to justify him: an old man on the rack who sees the Universe as a rack and finds no meaning in it. The part is unique and no actor ever completely succeeds in it: some explanation of its perhaps insurmountable difficulty may be found in the very nature of its abandonment to grief and pessimism: the whole thing is a dreadful epic of supermen " too huge for the stage." Certainly there is no other ending in Shakespeare of this nature. The old man, whatever his faults, deserved no such penalty; the customary army is on the stage, but nothing is said to assuage us. There is a bitterer ending in Shakespeare, but it is nothing near so annihilating as this. I mean the sneering recitation of Pandarus at the close of *Troilus and Cressida*. That is the one really ironic ending to a Shakespearean tragedy—and the irony is of the stage, though not so cheap as the ordinary modern ironic ending. Normally Shakespeare was above the exploitation of the ironic trick. Let irony reside in the nature of things, but he at least would not trade on it by easy contrasts of the dead great and the surviving paltry, anguish in a lonely room and the newsboys crying race-winners outside, or even, as a rule (this being on a higher scale), a turn of events coming just too late. No: the glorious with their one fatal fault, the wicked with their sustained guilt, his central tragic figures bring their fates upon them, and, when the axe has fallen, he is content to show life going on, and their surviving friends or enemies compassionately pronouncing their epitaphs. As Fortinbras's army marches in, a sign of continuity, so do other armies: the point of the fable has been made, the other point that life, even happy life, does not terminate with the greatest protagonist, is made also; at long last our sense of proportion is restored. As for the dead wicked, they have ceased from troubling; as for the dead weary, they are at rest. " Let's make the best of it," says the Second Lord after Coriolanus has been assassinated, and we have admitted (however violently resisting) that he got his due. *Romeo and Juliet* concludes with a family reconciliation and the prospect of a monument: something, at least, for mankind those unhappy lovers have done. "This happy day," on the complacent lips of Octavius, are the last words of *Julius Cæsar*—Octavius, who actually "saw out" two of the tragedies. "The noblest Roman of them all" has perished on his own sword; but, though noble, he courted Nemesis, and Rome, whose security he threatened whilst meaning to save it, goes on. After Othello's tragedy there is less assuagement, though at least a worldly justice awaits "the Spartan dog" and honour from the State is in store for Othello. In *Macbeth* we are less troubled. Here the heroes are actually the villains: we happen to have become deeply engaged with them as we have been privy to their excitements, their agonies, their great poetry. But when Fortinbras-Malcolm rings down the curtain on them, we view them from the outside, and realize that there is truth in his blunt verdict on "this dead butcher and his fiend-like queen." She was more fiend than he was butcher!

> *Macb.:* I have done the deed. Did'st thou not hear a noise?
> *Lady M.:* I heard the owl scream and the crickets cry.
> Did you not speak?
> *Macb.:*   When?
> *Lady M.:*   Now.
> *Macb.:*   As I descended?
> *Lady M.:* Ay.

> *Macb.:* Hark!
> Who lies i' the second chamber?
> *Lady M.:* Donalbain.
> *Macb.* (*looking on his hands*): This is a sorry sight.
> *Lady M.:* A foolish thought to say a sorry sight.
> *Macb.:* There's one did laugh in's sleep, and one cried ' Murder! '
> That they did wake each other: I stood and heard them;
> But they did say their prayers, and address'd them
> Again to sleep.
> *Lady M.:* There are two lodged together.
> *Macb.:* One cried ' God bless us! ' and ' Amen! ' the other:
> As they had seen me with these hangman's hands.
> Listening their fear, I could not say ' Amen,'
> When they did say ' God bless us! '
> *Lady M.:* Consider it not so deeply.

It is simply like the early chapters of Genesis all over again.

Detached though Shakespeare may have been, of a sceptical habit and prone to the contemplation of mortality, he did not, after this tragic theme was worked out, load the dice at the end and leave his hearer in a mood for bitter blasphemy or a flight from life. It was life he showed, nothing less nor worse: he had a temper which prompted him to long views, and remembered laughter in hours of anguish, if also he held a memory of pain and death when kisses were light and the cup went round. The statement that " he saw life whole " is never better borne out than by the last speeches of his tragedies: he would not stoop to the advocacy of pessimism—nor of optimism either.

CHAPTER V

THE DRAMATIC PRESENTATION OF CHARACTER

VARIOUS means of displaying character are open to the novelist, whether dramatic or other; but a dramatic writer employs them otherwise, and in different proportions, than does the novelist. Before we come to Shakespeare's methods and achievements in this regard, it would be best briefly to consider the possibilities open to him and the restrictions under which he (and the modern playwright is even more rigidly cribbed, cabined and confined) had to work.

Roughly, I suppose, we may take it that there are six ways in which an author (whether dramatic or not) may indicate the nature of a character.

(1) By describing or exhibiting his dress and facial expression.

(2) By exhibiting him in action or conflict—but all action is conflict with something or somebody.

(3) By making him express ideas and emotions in speech.

(4) By giving him a 'characteristic' method of expressing himself—tone, vocabulary, pace, degree of education and peculiar propensity of imagery and incidental information.

(5) By telling us what is going on in his mind.

THE DRAMATIC PRESENTATION OF CHARACTER 139

(6) By letting us hear what other people think about him.

All these methods can be employed by both the dramatist and the novelist, and Shakespeare employed them all effectively. But the dramatist has certain advantages over the novelist, and the novelist over the dramatist.

The supreme advantage of the novelist lies in the fact that he is under no restrictions of length. It is a substantial play that runs to twenty thousand words: the ordinary novel of commerce runs to seventy or a hundred thousand; some of the great novels have run to half a million. With the novelist no refinement of description or direct revelation need be spared. The dramatist must be concise, ruthlessly selective; everything has to be cut to the bone; his nails have to be driven in with single blows.

The second great advantage that the novelist has is that he can tell us as much as he likes about what is going on in his characters' minds; in fact, some modern novels contain hardly any dialogue at all and reveal both their characters and their plots entirely by describing the flow of consciousness. Shakespeare had an equivalent to this in the soliloquy, which was a conventional device, not meant to be regarded as realistic, whereby the author told us what a character was thinking, not what he ever would have dreamt of saying aloud, even when by himself. But this device could, in the nature of plays, only be used sparingly; and was, except in *Hamlet* and *Othello*, used very sparingly indeed. It would take a Pirandello to write a play composed entirely of soliloquies and asides, and only an extremely sophisticated audience would stand it. The normal modern playwright, having abandoned the soliloquy as unconvincing, has no substitute for the novelist's habit of exposing his characters' unspoken thoughts; but Shakespeare had, to a very limited extent.

But, from our present point of view, the playwright has one quite immense advantage over the novelist. The simulacra of his characters are present to our eyes from first to last. He may even, if (as Shakespeare often did) he writes his plays for particular actors, be saved entirely the task of conceiving their personal appearance, and, in part, of conceiving their minds and tempers. Anybody who deliberately wrote a play centred round the late Sir Henry Irving would not hesitate as to whether his central character could look and behave like Mr. George Robey. He need describe nobody's face (unless he cares to insert in his natural dialogue such a guide to producers as: "Yon Cassius has a lean and hungry look") for the face is evident to the audience, and doing instantaneously (assisted by make-up) with eyes, eyebrows, nose, mouth, jaws, shoulders, arms, hands and legs what the novelist has to be at great pains to describe. He need not bother to tell us about scenery. In Shakespeare's day a few properties and brief allusions did all that was required. In

THE DRAMATIC PRESENTATION OF CHARACTER 141

our own day not a word (the rights and wrongs of the matter are discussed elsewhere) need necessarily be said about scenery and weather, as they are palpable. The programme says 'Early Dawn'; the Globe-Wernicke (or whatever) system of lighting dutifully produces the Roseate Hues; and the Dramatis Personæ can get on with their business. The novelist, however, whether using nature as mere picturesque backgrounds or whether (following the sensible footsteps of Shakespeare, who knew that Theatre was Theatre) exploiting the Pathetic Fallacy for all he is worth, or whether urged merely by a desire to express his poetic response to the majesties and the lovelinesses of the world around us, must expend a great deal of his time in writing about 'settings.' Thomas Hardy's masterpiece, *The Return of the Native*, opens with that prolonged, glorious, imagination-stirring, mind-stirring, heart-stirring, description of Egdon Heath. A dramatist would have no time for it, but no need for it. An Elizabethan audience could see it with the mind's eye, assisted by a sentence such as Gloucester's about that other heath:

> Alack! the night comes on, and the high winds
> Do sorely ruffle; for many miles about
> There's scarce a bush.

From Hardy's own works the contrast could be illustrated. His *Tess of the D'Urbervilles*, full, like all his novels, of noble descriptive passages, was turned into a play—a touching and interesting if amateurish play—and produced at Kew. A curtain rose: a simple downland backcloth and a signpost suggested all the smoothness, greenness, vastness, loneliness and antiquity of Salisbury Plain. In the novel these qualities have to be driven in by iteration, by elaborate description to begin with and constant reminders afterwards. On the stage the scene is there and visible as long as it is wanted: we need no reminder because we can see it. But in the novel we demand, and get, this sort of thing:

She plunged into the chilly equinoctial darkness as the clock struck ten, for her fifteen miles' walk under the steely stars. In lonely districts night is a protection rather than a danger to a noiseless pedestrian, and knowing this, Tess pursued the nearest course along by-lanes that she would almost have feared in the daytime; but marauders were wanting now, and spectral fears were driven out of her mind by thoughts of her mother. Thus she proceeded mile after mile, ascending and descending till she came to Bulbarrow, and about midnight looked from that height into the abyss of chaotic shade which was all that revealed itself of the vale on whose further side she was born. Having already traversed about five miles on the upland she had now some ten or eleven in the lowland before her journey would be finished. The winding road downwards became just visible to her under the wan starlight as she followed it, and soon she paced a soil so contrasting with that above it that the difference was perceptible to the tread and to the smell. It was the heavy clay land of Blackmoor Vale, and a part of the Vale to which turnpike-roads had never penetrated. Superstitions linger longest on these heavy soils. Having once been forest, at this shadowy time it seemed to assert something of its old character, the far and the near being blended, and every tree and tall hedge making the most of its presence. The harts that had been hunted here, the witches that had been pricked and ducked, the green-spangled fairies that ' whickered ' at you as you passed; the place teemed with beliefs in them still, and they formed an impish multitude now.

Suppose, as a further illustration, that somebody tried to adapt a typical novel of Conrad's (say *The Rescue*) to the stage. He would find, as he sorted out dialogue and action from description, that, for drama, the book was a short story about people and a long, if exquisitely beautiful, story about hot skies, palms and jungles, sluggish muddy rivers, oily pearly seas, dawn, sunset, night and the stars—all of it, on the stage, barely though adequately suggestible in dialogue, and if done elaborately only to be done with scenery, which occupies space but no time. Herein lies a great compensation to the dramatist, who has but a " three-hours' traffic " while the novelist's readers can lay him down and resume him after a week or month, and the novelist himself can expatiate as long as he likes, and can even be skimmed, as a play cannot be skimmed. " Sleep is also a form of criticism," said the French dramatic critic; and it is an advantage to the novelist that one can go to sleep over a novel and pick it up again after the operative longueur, whereas once one has gone to sleep in the theatre the play is anyhow done for, and very likely all over before one wakes up. As against this, if I may repeat myself, the playwright has the signal advantage that he is saved endless trouble about describing scenery; and, in respect to character, all that trouble which is expended by the novelist on describing his peoples' clothes, gaits, voices, gestures and facial expressions. The dramatist does not have to say: " Suddenly Iago came in, clad in black from top to toe, rapier on hip. There was something feline about his movements, and something foxy about the smile on his intellectual but cruel face, as he stood removed from the unsuspecting others, and whispered revengefully to himself." There is an actor on the stage to do all that; and, by his physical recurrence, perpetually to remind us of it.

Those differences allowed, and the fact emphasized that the dramatist (except in so far as he may slenderly explain people's characters by the commentary of soliloquy and the commentary of other people's observations) has mainly to rely upon the direct speech and action of his persons, we may consider how Shakespeare, with the slight means at a playwright's disposal, conveyed so unerringly characters so complete that we seem to know many of them, such as Falstaff, Brutus and Othello, as well as our most intimate friends.

Pope, in an age when the greatness of Shakespeare was just beginning to be realized, and one

THE DRAMATIC PRESENTATION OF CHARACTER 145

which was by no means sympathetic to his music or his romanticism of outlook, uttered, in this connection, a panegyric which even Coleridge or Swinburne could not have surpassed:

His Characters are so much Nature herself that 'tis a sort of injury to call them by so distant a name as Copies of her. Those of other Poets have a constant resemblance, which shews that they received them from one another and were but multiplyers of the same image: each picture like a mock-rainbow is but the reflexion of a reflexion. But every single character in Shakespear is as much an Individual, as those in Life itself; it is as impossible to find any two alike; and such as from their relation or affinity in any respect appear most to be Twins, will upon comparison be found remarkably distinct. To this life and variety of Character, we must add the wonderful Presentation of it; which is such throughout his plays, that had all the Speeches been printed without the very names of the Persons, I believe one might have apply'd them with certainty to every speaker.

This, of course, like every such deliriously enthusiastic eulogy, cannot be taken quite literally. So far as the major characters in Shakespeare are concerned (and this will be emphasized in a later chapter) it is certainly true to say that we should know who was speaking even were the names not given. But even Shakespeare could not be bothered always to give distinctive personalities to the filling-up, vehicular, cementing and conjoining characters of the type known to the last age as: 'Charles, his Friend.' An actor once confided in me that he was annoyed with always being cast for 'silly-ass' parts when he could do other things adequately, if not better. I knew what those parts were, a compost of mannerisms interchangeable from play to play. In the Restoration plays—apart from those of Congreve and the less lively and libidinous works of Dryden—which Pope probably had in mind when he wrote about 'Twins,' there are countless Lord Foppingtons and such, which are not many but one. Shakespeare never repeated his characters quite so flagrantly as that; but there were occasions when the veriest sketch sufficed him, and a nominal character was only present as a useful agent or foil. Pinned to his point, Pope could hardly have insisted on maintaining that the Gratianos, Roderigos, all the dozens of gentlemen of Verona, Venice and elsewhere, were distinct, complete, and unique as are Lear and Ancient Pistol. Even Horatio, I suspect, is only real to us, not because of anything he says, but because Hamlet obviously thinks him a good, generous, utterly loyal man. "The truth is," said Coleridge, "Shakespeare's characters are all *genera* intensely individualized"—an observation supplemented by his later remark: "In *Lear* old age is itself a character." But on occasion, I think, the genus was left as it stood.

Yet, in the main—and one is bound to exaggerate, in the heat of the moment, when comparing

THE DRAMATIC PRESENTATION OF CHARACTER 147

Shakespeare's powers of character-creation with those of all other writers, and especially those of all other dramatists—Pope is right. Characters swarmed from Shakespeare's brain as (though mostly in the easier form of caricatures) they swarmed from Dickens's; and he had an unparalleled power, by virtue of imagination, genius and craftsman's cunning, of making them comprehensible and memorable in a few sentences, of giving the mind the significant bones from which the whole skeleton could be automatically deduced.

The description of people's characters through the mouths of others was a very favourite device of his. The plays are sprinkled with such things, and they never fail. Naturally, the words have to be related to those who speak; if an Iago gives a malignant description of Othello, we know (knowing Iago) that Othello will have none of the thoughts imputed to him—yet any account of a man by anybody whose own character and motives we know must be useful towards the formation of a complete character of him. Normally and naturally, these descriptions, usually as true as they are illuminating, are delivered when the people described are off-stage. But in at least one notable instance light of this kind is thrown when the person referred to is present. In *The Winter's Tale*, IV. 3, the Shepherd, with Perdita and all sorts of guests there and a feast imminent which needs a mistress, gives us, as an address to Perdita, precisely the sort of indication of her modesty, sweetness and charm as he might have given (but being young she can only reply with an assent) had she been off the stage and he telling other people about her:

> *Shep:* Fie, daughter! when my old wife liv'd, upon
> This day she was both pantler, butler, cook;
> Both dame and servant; welcom'd all, serv'd all,
> Would sing her song and dance her turn; now here,
> At the upper end o' the table, now i' the middle;
> On his shoulder, and his; her face o' fire
> With labour and the thing she took to quench it,
> She would to each one sip. You are retired,
> As if you were a feasted one and not
> The hostess of the meeting: pray you, bid
> These unknown friends to's welcome; for it is
> A way to make us better friends, more known.
> Come, quench your blushes and present yourself
> That which you are, mistress o' the feast: come on,
> And bid us welcome to your sheep-shearing,
> As your good flock shall prosper.

In one small speech two characters are surely drawn. There is the dead old wife, buxom, gay, hospitable, friendlily bibulous at feasts, apple-cheeked: possibly an inhabitant of 'Bohemia' (which to Shakespeare was Erewhon or Ruritania) but certainly an inhabitant of Arden or a 'Cotsall' dame, and certainly the kind of old country-woman, as lavish at feasts, whether with pipe and tabor, or serpent and fiddle, as she had to be frugal (though always with something in reserve for gossip or stranger) as the old women Thomas Hardy remembered dancing the old country-dances in Dorset, and I myself can remember existing in West Devon and Cornwall before Harvest-Homes, sharp cider, local song and clotted cream went out, and American music, separators, education for all, town-domination, Canadian Cheddar, Canadian apples, frozen Argentine beef, ' Canterbury ' lamb, tinned goods, multiple stores, rustless (and edgeless) steel set in. That dead old shepherd's wife—who might have been a character in Hardy's *Three Wayfarers*—though dead, is present; but so also, with the slightest of indications, is Perdita, young, shrinking, reluctant, but willing, if enjoined by the kind old man, to fill, in her inexperienced way, the place of the jolly old dame now gone. After her reply there is no more to be said, it so bears out her modesty, innocence and willingness:

> *Perdita:*   Sir, welcome:
> It is my father's will I should take on me
>   The hostess-ship o' the day. (*To Camillo*)
>   You're welcome, sir.
> Give me those flowers there, Dorcas. Reverend sirs,
> For you there's rosemary and rue; these keep
> Seeming and savour all the winter long:
> Grace and remembrance be to you both,
> And welcome to our shearing!

We know all of her after that: the shepherd and herself with a speech each.

Another variant of the descriptive speech about a character off-stage is the sparsely-used description, by himself, of a person on-stage, who talks about himself as dispassionately as though he were talking about somebody else. A prime example is that of Menenius in *Coriolanus*:

> *Men.:* I am known to be a humorous patrician, and one that loves a cup of hot wine with not a drop of allaying Tiber in't; said to be something imperfect in favouring the first complaint; hasty and tinder-like upon too trivial motion; one that converses more with the buttock of the night than with the forehead of the morning. What I think I utter, and spend my malice in my breath. Meeting two such weals-men as you are,—I cannot call you Lycurguses,—if the drink you give me touch my palate adversely, I make a crooked face at it.

It is extremely unlikely that any man would give such a convincing and honest account of himself (an account which could easily be transposed by substituting ' he ' for ' I ' and ' his ' and ' my '): but it does the job and perhaps there is a little added touch given by the fact that Menenius himself produces the diagnosis instead of leaving it for somebody else to produce behind his back.

These, however, are variants, and rare. Such little summaries and indications of character are usually put by Shakespeare into the mouths of friends, enemies or merely neutral watchers when the people talked about are off the stage, and very often, as exciting preparation, before they have ever appeared on it.

A few typical examples must suffice. There is Benedick about Beatrice, whom he is destined to abuse, cross swords with, and marry still on the note of badinage, though love be palpably underneath it:

She told me, not thinking I had been myself, that I was the prince's jester; that I was duller than a great thaw; huddling jest upon jest with such impossible conveyance upon me, that I stood like a man at a mark, with a whole army shooting at me. She speaks poniards, and every word stabs: if her breath were as terrible as her terminations, there were no living near her; she would infect to the north star. I would not marry her, though she were endowed with all that Adam had left him before he transgressed; she would have made Hercules have turned spit, yea, and have cleft his club to make the fire too. Come, talk not of her; you shall find her the infernal Ate in good apparel. I would to God some scholar would conjure her, for certainly, while she is here, a man may live as quiet in hell as in a sanctuary; and people sin upon purpose because they would go thither; so, indeed, all disquiet, horror and perturbation follow her.

Do we need any more to prepare us for her immediate entry: " Will your Grace command me any service to the world's end ? " The witty, difficult, giving-nothing-away intellectual minx is all there; she is a female Benedick, or Mercutio (who was very like Benedick but died by misfortune instead of falling into a lover's arms) and a match for Benedick, and destined to fall (though fall is hardly the word) into his arms with the score ' quits,' or ' love-all,' whichever you may choose to call it. A shorter indication is Berowne's in *Love's Labour's Lost*:

> This is the ape of form, monsieur the nice,
> That, when he plays at tables, chides the dice
> In honourable terms.

No more need be said: we know the kind, and the person on the stage can never recover from it. In *A Midsummer-Night's Dream*, again:

> *Hel.:* O! when she's angry, she is keen and shrewd.
> She was a vixen when she went to school:
> And though she be but little, she is fierce.

There is an elaboration of this device of displaying off-stage characters through the comment of on-stage characters in *The Merchant of Venice* when Portia talks to Nerissa about her extremely ineligible stream of suitors. This is a selection only:

> *Ner.:* How say you by the French lord, Monsieur Le Bon?
> *Por.:* God made him, and therefore let him pass for a man. In truth, I know it is a sin to be a mocker; but he! why, he hath a horse better than the Neapolitan's, a better bad habit

THE DRAMATIC PRESENTATION OF CHARACTER 153

of frowning than the Count Palatine; he is every man in no man; if a throstle sing, he falls straight a-capering; he will fence with his own shadow: if I should marry him, I should marry twenty husbands. If he would despise me, I would forgive him, for if he love me to madness, I shall never requite him.

Ner.: What say you then to Falconbridge, the young baron of England?

Por.: You know I say nothing to him, for he understands not me, nor I him: he hath neither Latin, French, nor Italian, and you will come into the court and swear that I have a poor pennyworth in the English. He is a proper man's picture, but, alas! who can converse with a dumbshow? . . .

In the same play Shylock is characterized off-stage by Salarino, one of those useful but nugatory personages who defeat Pope's dictum:

> I never heard a passion so confused,
> So strange, outrageous, and so variable,
> As the dog Jew did utter in the streets:
> ' My daughter! O my ducats! O my daughter!
> Fled with a Christian! O my Christian ducats!
> Justice! the law! my ducats, and my daughter!
> A sealed bag, two sealed bags of ducats,
> Of double ducats, stol'n from me by my daughter!'

Polixenes in *The Winter's Tale* describes the King:

Pol.: The king hath on him such a countenance

> As he had lost some province and a region
> Lov'd as he loves himself: even now I met him
> With customary compliment, when he,
> Wafting his eyes to the contrary, and falling
> A lip of much contempt, speeds from me and
> So leaves me to consider what is breeding
> That changes thus his manners.

Would not jealousy be obvious from that, even did we not know it before from that ghastly speech, far nastier than anything which ever poor deluded Othello said, which begins: " Is whispering nothing ? "

In *Richard III* we find a whole characterization of the absent Hastings in Gloucester's lines:

> Catesby hath sounded Hastings in our business,
> And finds the testy gentleman so hot,
> That he will lose his head ere give consent
> His master's child, as worshipfully he terms it,
> Shall lose the royalty of England's throne.

Briefer still, and equally indicative, is the first description of Ajax in *Troilus and Cressida*. Alexander says:

> They say he is a very man *per se*
> And stands alone.

It is said in Latin by a Greek, but 'twill serve. In *Timon of Athens*, in the very first scene occur these lines:

> Yea, from the glass-faced flatterer,
> To Apemantus, that few things loves better
> Than to abhor himself.

THE DRAMATIC PRESENTATION OF CHARACTER 155

In *Julius Cæsar*, II. 1, Brutus says of Cicero, who is being considered as a possible conspirator:

> O! name him not: let us not break with him;
> For he will never follow any thing
> That other men begin.

Whole characters are there suggested in a word or two. We never know more about Macbeth than we are told by Lady Macbeth when she exclaims:

> Glamis thou art, and Cawdor; and shalt be
> What thou art promis'd. Yet do I fear thy
>   nature;
> It is too full o' the milk of human kindness
> To catch the nearest way; thou wouldst be
>   great,
> Art not without ambition, but without
> The illness should attend it; what thou wouldst
>   highly
> That thou wouldst holily; wouldst not play
>   false,
> And yet wouldst wrongly win; thou'dst have,
>   great Glamis,
> That which cries, 'Thus thou must do, if thou
>   have it';
> And that which rather thou dost fear to do
> Than wishest should be undone. Hie thee
>   hither,
> That I may pour my spirits in thine ear,
> And chastise with the valour of my tongue
> All that impedes thee from the golden round,
> Which fate and metaphysical aid doth seem
> To have thee crown'd withal.

In one small soliloquy she indicates both her husband's character and her own: he had his canons but was bewitched by her. It is almost evident from that speech that not only was he brave and weak, but that she was almost preternaturally beautiful and plausible; otherwise, why should his standards have gone, which ultimately led to him melting into butter inside his armour, conscience not making a coward of him, but a stricken and beaten, although still courageous man?

Cleopatra is, more than almost any character in Shakespeare, described off-stage—with the signal help of Plutarch. But none of the elaborate descriptions of her, sailing down the Cydnus in a boat, fanned by peacocks' feathers, or hopping fifty paces along the public street and being enchanting even when panting after the unwonted exercise, is so forcible and final as Antony's single sentence:

> She is cunning, past man's thought.

But to illustrate Shakespeare's production and development of character by direct speech and action would be to reproduce the plays bodily. A few examples only, in each kind, can be given. There is Dogberry:

> *Dog.:* Dost thou not suspect my place? Dost thou not suspect my years? O! that he were here to write me down an ass! but, masters, remember that I am an ass; though it be not written down, yet forget not that I am an ass.

No, thou villain, thou art full of piety, as shall be proved upon thee by good witness. I am a wise fellow; and, which is more, an officer; and which is more, a householder; and, which is more, as pretty a piece of flesh as any in Messina; and one that knows the law, go to; and a rich fellow enough, go to; and a fellow that hath had losses; and one that hath two gowns, and everything handsome about him. Bring him away. O! that I had been writ down an ass!

There is Regan again, in a horrible line and a half after Gloucester has been blinded:

> *Regan:* Go thrust him out at gates and let him smell
> His way to Dover.

There is Henry VI in almost the only speech in all his plays which at once reveals his character and confesses Shakespeare's hand:

> *King Hen.:* I have not stopp'd mine ears to their demands,
> Nor posted off their suits with slow delays;
> My pity hath been balm to heal their wounds,
> My mildness hath allay'd their swelling griefs,
> My mercy dried their water-flowing tears;
> I have not been desirous of their wealth,
> Nor much oppress'd them with great subsidies,
> Nor forward of revenge, though they much err'd.
> Then why should they love Edward more than me?

How instantly we see the founder of Eton and King's, the patron and colleague of the great musician John of Dunstable, astray and bewildered in a century of cruel baronial wars! Little Prince Arthur, again—as it were a young Henry VI, in another age of civil strife:

> By my christendom,
> So I were out of prison and kept sheep,
> I should be as merry as the day is long:
> And so I would be here, but that I doubt
> My uncle practises more harm to me.

Falstaff and his crew, the Nurse in *Romeo and Juliet*, the Greeks in *Troilus and Cressida*: they all live as soon as they appear, and through speaking succinctly in character. Iago reveals himself so instantly in the very first scene of *Othello* that it is a pity his remarks are usually made while the audience is taking its seats:

> *Iago*: Despise me if I do not. Three great ones of the city,
> In personal suit to make me his lieutenant,
> Off-capp'd to him; and, by the faith of man,
> I know my price, I am worth no worse a place;
> But he, as loving his own pride and purposes,
> Evades them, with a bombast circumstance
> Horribly stuff'd with epithets of war;
> And, in conclusion,
> Nonsuits my mediators; for, ' Certes,' says he,
> ' I have already chose my officer.'
> And what was he?
> Forsooth, a great arithmetician,

THE DRAMATIC PRESENTATION OF CHARACTER 159

> One Michael Cassio, a Florentine,
> A fellow almost damn'd in a fair wife;
> That never set a squadron in the field,
> Nor the division of a battle knows
> More than a spinster; unless the bookish theoric,
> Wherein the toged consuls can propose
> As masterly as he: mere prattle, without practice,
> Is all his soldiership. But he, sir, had the election;
> And I—of whom his eyes had seen the proof
> At Rhodes, at Cyprus, and on other grounds
> Christian and heathen—must be be-lee'd and calm'd
> By debitor and creditor; this counter-caster,
> He, in good time, must his lieutenant be,
> And I—God bless the mark!—his Moorship's ancient.

Character and motive are all there; the last touch of sneering being registered with the " his Moorship's "—which is almost a stage direction in itself.

Shakespeare's people, in the genuine plays, are seldom out of character, and seldom say anything which does not contribute towards our knowledge of them. Frequently also—though, as a rule, their acts are predestined by their characters—they suddenly *do* things which throw a blaze of light upon them. Perhaps the most illuminating action in the whole of the plays is Hamlet's sudden stabbing of Polonius, the rat behind the arras. From that we learn for a certainty that at a crisis—for instance, on a battlefield—the Prince of Denmark was a man of instant decisions who would fit the action to the word, and that it was only the peculiar situation in which he found himself, with only vague suspicions, instinctive dislike and a dubious ghost as evidence which sicklied him o'er with the pale cast of thought. In another world Jaques' action in offering to be best man to Touchstone and Audrey ("Proceed, proceed, I'll give her") throws equal light on the nearest thing to Hamlet that ever appeared in the comedies. The most melodramatic villain (in *Henry VI*, he is almost a Pecksniff) in Shakespeare grows to heroic stature with the one sentence: "A horse! A horse! My kingdom for a horse!" But if the whole evolution of a character through dialogue and action had to be studied, I should commend the student to that of Bertram in *All's Well That Ends Well*, that sulky, vain, attractive, handsome athlete, who as little deserved his Helena (though it is like life that he should get her) as Imogen's husband deserved Imogen.

CHAPTER VI

DIALOGUE AS REVEALING CHARACTER AND FORWARDING ACTION

In this chapter we shall consider the *words* in Shakespeare's plays irrespective of their existence in verse or prose, or their incidental beauty of sound or imagery. We shall examine them purely as dialogue, the two principal functions of which in a play are: (1) to forward the progress of the 'fable' in its widest sense, which includes the reactions and relations of the characters; and (2)—though this might be held to be part of the other—by the variety of its flow and content to express character itself and as fully as possible. A third function is to assist the actor: for, where other things are equal, that form of sentence should be prepared which makes it easy and natural for the actor to suit gesture to word. Mr. Granville-Barker, in his uniquely illuminating *Prefaces*, says:

The text of a play is a score waiting performance, and the performance and its preparation are, almost from the beginning, a work of collaboration. A producer may direct the preparation, certainly. But if he only knows how to give orders, he has mistaken his vocation; he had better be a drill-sergeant. He might talk to his company when they all met together for the first time to study *Love's Labour's Lost*, *Julius Cæsar* or *King Lear*, on some such lines as these prefaces pursue, giving a considered opinion of the play, drawing a picture of it in action, providing, in fact, a hypothesis which mutual study would prove—and might partly disprove. No sort of study of a play can better the preparation of its performance if this is rightly done. The art of the playwright lies in giving life to characters in action, and the secret of it in giving each character a due chance in the battle, the action of a play being literally the fighting of a battle of character. So the greater the playwright, the wider and deeper his sympathies, the more genuine this opposition will be and the less easily will a single mind grasp it, as it must be grasped, in the fullness of its emotion. The dialogue of a play runs—and often intricately—upon lines of reason, but it is charged besides with an emotion which speech releases, yet only releases fully when the speaker is—as an actor is—identified with the character. There is further the incidental action, implicit in the dialogue, which springs to life only when a scene is in being.

Those things here indicated are functions: an all-embracing condition is that dialogue, whatever it is doing, should be speakable on the stage, speakable so that the actor is not conscious of being too far from nature or too burdened with the need for making the obscure clear, and does not have his tongue tied up. The most lucid and limpid speech in the language is to be found in Shakespeare's plays. His standard is so high that when he merely mouths we can hardly believe it is he, and we hunt

DIALOGUE AS REVEALING CHARACTER

for explanations when we are confronted with such a slow and brain-racking thing as the Duke's first speech in *Measure for Measure:*

> *Duke:* Of government the properties to unfold,
> Would seem in me to affect speech and discourse,
> Since I am put to know that your own science
> Exceeds, in that, the lists of all advice
> My strength can give you: then no more remains,
> But that, to your sufficiency . . .

Unspeakable, and almost incomprehensible! But of these things later. It will be found that some of the considerations advanced here might well have found a place in one of the other chapters. A treatment of this subject—perhaps of most subjects —by chapters has its necessary defects: but if arbitrary, it is convenient.

No writer who ever lived has exhibited Shakespeare's range and certainty in the reproduction of the multitudinous characters of human speech. The word 'reproduction' needs qualification. No man's words, literally recorded over a period of more than a minute or so, would bear transference into a play. Complete realism in stage dialogue would be impossible; or if it be not impossible, would be intolerable. A great deal has to be done during "the three-hours' traffic of the stage," and the dialogue, suitably reinforced by the physical movements of persons and scenery, is there to do it:

sometimes in those hours, the quintessence of many years' events has to be communicated. Moreover, not only do human beings never speak with such sustained relevance, or with such compactness, as is necessary in stage dialogue, but they never speak so constantly in character as the persons of the stage must do if they are to give us the utmost possible entertainment and information about themselves. The character on the stage must be a sublimation of the character off the stage. All those idiosyncrasies and ' humours,' which we apprehend in our acquaintance as a result of long familiarity, must, in a play, be conveyed in a few short speeches in a few short scenes: the mirror is to be held up to nature, but it must be a mirror that intensifies.

The laconic man must be more demonstratively laconic than he ever is in life: not merely speaking habitually with preternatural concision, but withstanding provocations to volubility which in life even he could hardly resist. The bashful man must perpetually parade his shyness; the boastful must boast without intermission and on an heroic scale; the coward must be abandoned in his poltroonery; the wag must flow a very fountain of quips; the liar and the swearer must lie as Trojan never did, and swear like, perhaps, one titanic trooper in a thousand; the melancholy man must find sadness in stones and emblems of mortality in the running brooks; the lover must speak with the tongue of angels rather than of men, gathering into a single speech all the highest emotional sentences of an

DIALOGUE AS REVEALING CHARACTER   165

ordinary lifetime. This is true of all stage characters who are to be at all individualized, not remaining mere useful pieces of machinery like the servant who appears but to say, " Dinner is served," and then retires to seek his own supper. With characters of more importance, save only in the most artificial kind of comedy or farce, more has to be done than the mere emphasization, however entertaining, of the ' humour ' or the ' hobbyhorse ': the utmost possible light has to be shed, consistent with the proper conduct of the action, upon every aspect of them. The more completely we ' know ' them, the greater the dramatist's achievement, and the more they enrich the whole play that surrounds them: the more completely the dramatist knows them, the more they will help him to natural conclusions. They must ' react ' upon the predetermined main sequence of events, and that must revealingly affect them: situations and contacts must draw from them words which, while not obstructing the ' movement ' of the play, exhibit not only all the surface traits of their personalities, but even the secret motives of their actions, must even (if it be possible) make clear to us their motives and obscure predilections which are hidden from themselves. Probably no demagogue, from Demosthenes to Cicero, from Cicero to our own day, ever made a speech at once as immediately persuasive and as revelatory of his own character (in this instance both cunning and hearty) as Antony's after Cæsar's death: skilful utterly, truth indistinguishable from falsehood, the thing inspired by the audience indistinguishable from the thing felt from within. But if such a speech was never made, it is only because this speech embodies the concentrated truth about all such speeches: and Antony is exhibited in a few lines better than most orators are exhibited in whole volumes of their sophistical and emotional wind-baggery.

On the highest plane of dramatic characterization we find persons, such as Falstaff, Hamlet and even the brilliantly and briefly sketched Mercutio, from whose given words and deeds we can (or at least think we can) deduce all that is not told us, all that is not deliberately even indicated, the whole nature of their inner lives and the manner in which they would, by choice or of necessity, behave in any conceivable set of circumstances. As Pope said: " Had all the Speeches been printed without the names of the Persons, I believe one might have apply'd them with certainty to every speaker." When Brutus' Portia, who has no great place in the play, says:

> Tell me your counsels, I will not disclose 'em.
> I have made strong proof of my constancy,
> Giving myself a voluntary wound
> Here, in the thigh: can I bear that with patience
> And not my husband's secrets?

do we not know her? To do all this, in a play of from two to three thousand lines, for any given character, the dramatist has at his disposal but a few score, or a few hundred, or a few thousand words. He is precluded from describing his characters in his own person; he can only very sparingly describe their qualities through the mouths of their neighbours, who must not (merely for the convenience of an author) indulge in set accounts when they would not naturally do so; his medium is words spoken within the narrow boundaries set by plot, by the characters themselves who are to be made known to us. These facts borne in mind will help us to measure the prodigy of Shakespeare's achievement in creating a world full of people whom we know as well as our intimate friends, a world so large and variegated that there is no type of character not to be found there, and so vivid that it is more real to us than the actual Elizabethan background against which it was constructed. His characters had to be fitted into plot; he so loved and realized them that he often found it difficult to fit them into plot; but for all his struggles with such people as Falstaff and Othello, who had to be the swaggerer and the jealous man, we still know them, and think of them as merely lapsing out of character when they do not behave as we expect them to. What, honestly, are even Drake and Raleigh to us as against Hamlet and Othello? Queen Elizabeth herself, for all her sturdy sentences, her dyes, and ruffs, and crust of pearls, is dim compared with them: and the deeps of her unknown.

There is no parallel in literature to the range of Shakespeare's dialogue: the variety of accent and colour with which he discriminated between characters, the variety of dramatic effect which he secured by the modification of speech. And, since he was a man of the theatre and, as he wrote, heard each word spoken correctly, he often left a good deal to the sense of the actor which does not fully appear to the mere reader. "Mark," says Professor Baker acutely,

"when running through the scene in which Iago tempts Othello to his undoing (Act III, Scene 3) the variety of intonation required in the repetitions of 'honest' and 'think.' In a novel containing this scene the absence of the actors' trained intonations would cost the author much labour in describing how the words should be uttered."

The more laconically Shakespeare is writing, the more this is true. He was laconic at his greatest moments, resisting especially then (as few poets have ever been able to do) the temptation to rhetoric as well as the other strong temptation to 'prettify.'

His characters, major and minor, have habits of speech which are strongly individualized. There are exceptions, particularly in the early, and notably in the historical plays. Kings and potentates tend (though not unnaturally) to a uniform official dignity of utterance, and passages (suitable for recitation in schools, such as: "So work the honey bees") are put into one mouth that might as well have been put into another. But in general this masterly individualization of speech is Shakespeare's mark. Even the young Shakespeare of *Love's Labour's Lost*, though he was writing journalistic satire against ephemeral affectations and had still much to learn about the dramatic art, had already the knack (hardly a knack, for it arose from his strong sense of character) of introducing a person with a sentence strongly indicative of the whole man. Armado walks on with:

> Boy, what sign is it when a man of great spirit grows melancholy?

That one sentence tells us all about Armado and a great deal about Shakespeare, who suffered fools very gladly indeed.

Mr. Granville-Barker says:

> Plutarch's genius, in fact, is allied to Shakespeare's own, with its power to make, by a touch or so of nature, great men and simple, present and past, the real and the mimic world, one kin. . . . He redraws the outline of the story more simply but he cannot resist crowding characters in. What wonder, when they are all so striking, and he knows he can make a living man out of a dozen lines of dialogue.

His words characterized those who spoke them, and the rhythmic contours of their sentences often give us a sure indication of their whole tone and temper. He made the mood suit the action and the person. All Brutus is in the lines:

> I am not gamesome: I do lack some part
> Of that quick spirit that is in Antony.

But individualization, as in life, is at its highest mark with comic characters: we should know it was Falstaff talking did we but hear the wheedlings and swaggerings and jocular ripplings of his voice through a wall without distinguishing the words: and the words are written for him so that an actor can speak them in one way and no other.

Give me my robe, for I will go.

There are countless such passages in brief words, as Lear's:

Never, never, never, never, never.

About the only passage with which I quarrel in Mr. Granville-Barker's *Prefaces*—written by a man, author, actor, producer, who has excelled all the commentators on Shakespeare, most of them incapable of poetry, acting or producing—is one of these terse things. He says:

Edmund may be dying, but surely Shakespeare might rouse him, if he would, to something livelier than:

> This speech of yours hath mov'd me
> And shall, perchance, do good, but speak you on;
> You look as you had something more to say.

I challenge any actor to give colour to that last line.

I, on the other hand, suggest that Mr. Granville-Barker, either as actor or producer, could have

DIALOGUE AS REVEALING CHARACTER 171

given all the colour in the world to that last line.

Shakespeare had at his instant service words and tones to characterize every class and calling, every intellectual and emotional species, from carpenter to king, from drunken sot to ecstatic poet-lover. His debates between princes and Greek chieftains are as natural as his conversations between clowns; the crowd scenes in *Julius Cæsar* and *Coriolanus* (the last clinched with the bitter phrase " Rome and her rats ") owe their amazing realism to his power of compressing the thoughts of crowds into characteristic speech, whilst making all bear upon his main action. He commanded the whole gamut of expressive speech from the brief bitter conversations of Regan and Goneril, in which every sentence is like a physical blow, to the melancholy lamentations of Richard II, languorous to the point of lethargy and for music softer and sweeter than ' tir'd eyelids upon tir'd eyes."

Where, in dialogue, he obliterates the distinctions of character, it is usually because he is tempted to shed the graces of his own thought, provoked naturally enough, upon one who would not have thought as imaginatively as he, or imputes the graces of his own speech to one whom we cannot conceive as uttering the most ravishing music of which Shakespeare was capable. But at this point, examples of his variety will speak best: here are a few sentences illustrating the ease and certainty into which he made personality and mood express itself in fitting words. There is Constance's angry sarcasm:

> *Elinor:* Come to thy grandam, child.
> *Constance:* Do, child, go to it grandam, child;
> Give grandam kingdom, and it grandam will
> Give it a plum, a cherry, and a fig:
> There's a good grandam.

Here is Leontes, angry, proud and humourless:

> On your allegiance,
> Out of the chamber with her! Were I a tyrant,
> Where were her life? she durst not call me so
> If she did know me one. Away with her!

Richard III and his mother:

> *Duchess:* God bless thee! and put meekness in thy mind,
> Love, charity, obedience and true duty.
> *Gloucester:* Amen; (*aside*) and make me die a good old man!
> That is the butt-end of a mother's blessing;
> I marvel that her Grace did leave it out.

Cressida and Pandarus:

> *Cressida:* O Jupiter! there's no comparison.
> *Pandarus:* What! not between Troilus and Hector? Do you know a man if you see him?
> *Cres.:* Ay, if I ever saw him before and knew him.

DIALOGUE AS REVEALING CHARACTER 173

> *Pand.:* Well, I say Troilus is Troilus.
> *Cres.:* Then you say as I say; for I am sure he is not Hector.
> *Pand.:* No, nor Hector is not Troilus in some degrees.
> *Cres.:* 'Tis just to each of them; he is himself.
> *Pand.:* Himself! Alas! poor Troilus, I would he were. . . .
> *Cres.:* He is not Hector.
> *Pand.:* Himself! no, he's not himself. Would a' were himself: well, the gods are above; time must friend or end: well, Troilus, well, I would my heart were in her body. No, Hector is not a better man than Troilus.

Lady Capulet and the Nurse:

> *Nurse:* She is not fourteen. How long is it now to Lammas-tide?
> *Lady C.:* A fortnight and odd days.
> *Nurse:* Even or odd, of all days in the year, Come Lammas-eve at night shall she be fourteen.
> Susan and she—God rest all Christian souls!—
> Were of an age. Well, Susan is with God;
> She was too good for me. But, as I said,
> On Lammas-eve at night shall she be fourteen;
> That shall she, marry; I remember it well.
> 'Tis since the earthquake now eleven years;
> And she was wean'd, I never shall forget it,
> Of all the days of the year, upon that day;
> For I had then laid wormwood to my dug,
> Sitting in the sun under the dove-house wall;
> My lord and you were then at Mantua.
> Nay, I do bear a brain:—but as I said . . .

Caliban, Trinculo and Stephano—drunk:

> *Stephano:* Moon-calf, speak once in thy life, if thou beest a good moon-calf.
> *Caliban:* How does thy honour? Let me lick thy shoe. I'll not serve him; he is not valiant.
> *Trinculo:* Thou liest, most ignorant monster: I am in case to justle a constable. Why, thou deboshed fish, thou, was there ever a man a coward that hath drunk so much sack as I to-day? Wilt thou tell a monstrous lie, being but half a fish and half a monster?
> *Cal.:* Lo, how he mocks me! Wilt thou let him, my lord?
> *Trin.:* ' Lord ' quoth he! That a monster should be such a natural!
> *Cal.:* Lo, lo, again! bite him to death, I prithee.
> *Steph.:* Trinculo, keep a good tongue in your head: if you prove a mutineer, the next tree! The poor monster's my subject, and he shall not suffer indignity.

Sir Toby, intoxicated, a brief appearance:

> *Olivia:* By mine honour, half drunk. What is he at the gate, cousin?
> *Sir Toby:* A gentleman.
> *Olivia:* A gentleman! what gentleman?
> *Sir Toby:* 'Tis a gentleman here,—a plague of these pickle herring! How now, sot!
> *Clown:* Good Sir Toby.
> *Olivia:* Cousin, cousin, how have you come so early by this lethargy?

Sir Toby: Lechery! I defy lechery. There's one at the gate.
Olivia: Ay, marry, what is he?
Sir Toby: Let him be the devil, an he will, I care not: give me faith, say I. Well, it's all one. (*Exit.*)

Falstaff, mollifying and borrowing money from the poor aggrieved Dame Quickly:

Falstaff: As I am a gentleman.
Dame Quickly: Nay, you said so before.
Fal.: As I am a gentleman. Come, no more words of it.
Quick.: By this heavenly ground I tread on, I must be fain to pawn both my plate and the tapestry of my dining-chambers.
Fal.: Glasses, glasses, is the only drinking: and for thy walls, a pretty slight drollery, or the story of the Prodigal, or the German hunting in water-work, is worth a thousand of these bed-hangings and these fly-bitten tapestries. Let it be ten pound if thou canst. Come, an 'twere not for thy humours, there is not a better wench in England. Go, wash thy face, and draw thy action. Come, thou must not be in this humour with me; dost not know me? Come, come, I know thou wast set on to this.
Quick.: Prithee, Sir John, let it be but twenty nobles: i' faith, I am loath to pawn my plate, so God save me, la!
Fal.: Let it alone; I'll make other shift: you'll be a fool still.

Quick.: Well, you shall have it, though I pawn my gown. I hope you'll come to supper. You'll pay me altogether?

Fal.: Will I live? (*To Bardolph.*) Go, with her, with her; hook on, hook on.

All this, incidentally, does " our dear and ever honoured Sir John " (as Swinburne in his unqualified tribute called him) say aside while there still stands on the stage the Chief Justice, who has just rebuked him in set and sonorous phrases that admirably characterize the judge, from the reproving repetition of the first words to the lawyer-like termination:

Sir John, Sir John, I am well acquainted with your manner of wrenching the true cause the false way. It is not a confident brow, nor the throng of words that come with such more than impudent sauciness from you, can thrust me from a level consideration; you have, as it appears to me, practised upon the easy-yielding spirit of this woman, and made her serve your uses both in purse and in person.

We can even guess, underneath the lectures of this severe magistrate, the amusement that he represses; he will, in his restrained way, chuckle over the man and the episode when he is ' off-duty ' and having a night-cap with an old friend or two.

In almost the whole of these extracts the vocabulary is normal. The effect of individuality is not achieved (as Shakespeare could so supremely achieve

DIALOGUE AS REVEALING CHARACTER

it) by dialect, the use of low or affected terms, foreign accents or a profusion of tropes. The shading is subtle, and mainly obtained by construction, cadence and pace. Shakespeare's ear took in the finest distinctions and his imitative faculty enabled him automatically to reproduce them as though he heard every kind of person speak to him whilst he was in the act of writing. He compressed all the grand sonorities, all the grave sweetnesses, all the lusty ejaculations, and all the pretty titterings: every vocal note whether of Milton, or of Congreve, or of Dickens, or of Keats. He could turn with ease from the prophetic eloquence of Prospero, the spirited ranting of Henry V, the slow introspection of Hamlet, to the disconnected burblings of drunkards, the dainty clatter of shepherdesses, the broad rumblings of rustics, and the tiny pertnesses of fairies. With what a vocabulary Beatrice rattles on!

Leonato: You may light on a husband that hath no beard.

Beatrice: What should I do with him? dress him in my apparel and make him my waiting-gentlewoman? He that hath a beard is more than a youth, and he that hath no beard is less than a man; and he that is more than a youth is not for me; and he that is less than a man, I am not for him: therefore I will even take sixpence in earnest of the bear-ward, and lead his apes [1] into hell.

Leon.: Well then, go you into hell?

---
[1] A phrase meaning to be an old maid.

> *Beat.:* No; but to the gate; and there will the devil meet me, like an old cuckold, with horns on his head, and say ' Get you to heaven, Beatrice, get you to heaven; here's no place for you maids '; so deliver I up my apes, and away to St. Peter for the heavens; he shows me where the bachelors sit, and there live we as merry as the day is long.

Rosalind's banter of Orlando is as light and swift as Beatrice's, yet the gentler, gayer character differentiates it, and when she is left alone with Celia her love flows out between a smile and a sigh in an exquisite little torrent of words:

> *Ros.:* O coz, coz, coz, my pretty little coz, that thou didst know how many fathom deep I am in love! But it cannot be sounded: my affection hath an unknown bottom, like the bay of Portugal.

A sentence or two more and the scene ends:

> *Ros.:* I'll go find a shadow and sigh till he come.
> *Cel.:* And I'll sleep.

Sense and fantasy, humour and romance are mingled in a few contrasted words. The effect of contrast is stronger when not merely states of mind but deep differences of outlook or social condition are involved. Shakespeare constantly delights us by the mere juxtaposition of the speech of aristocrats and plebeians, drunk men and sober men, pompous men and flippant men, pedants and the unlearned—as with Leonato and Dogberry, Hamlet and the gravediggers, Malvolio and his tormentors. The effect of such contrast passes from piquancy to sublimity, when Shakespeare interposes colloquial jokes between the agonies of a distraught soul, not for 'comic relief' but for intensification by the comic, as in the dreadful jests of the Fool wandering with the raving Lear, and that earlier dialogue between them where Lear, after struggling to keep himself on the Fool's level of pathetic jocularity, suddenly cries out: 'O let me not be mad, not mad, sweet heaven,' and the effect is like the breaking of an abscess.

Shakespeare was a master of volubility, and could make every word in a torrent tell; a master also of the sustained declamation holding the audience by its force and passion or picturesqueness, and of the elaborate analytical passage. But nowhere in literature can such effective laconic dialogue be found as in his plays—in fact the presence or absence of such might well be one of the tests applied to doubtful plays. An example of both aptitudes is Brutus' oration, which closes with the terse, dramatic and proverbial: 'I pause for a reply.' He can, on occasion, convey whole characters and a whole situation by the mere repetition, in various inevitable tones, of a single word:

Lear: What can you say to draw a third more opulent than your sisters? Speak.
Cordelia: Nothing, my lord.

> *Lear:* Nothing ?
> *Cordelia:* Nothing.
> *Lear:* Nothing will come of nothing: speak again.

Later, Lear finds Kent put in the stocks by Regan:

> *Lear:* What's he that hath thy place so much mistook
> To set thee here ?
> *Kent:* It is both he and she,
> Your son and daughter.
> *Lear:* No.
> *Kent:* Yes.
> *Lear:* No, I say.
> *Kent:* I say, yea.
> *Lear:* No, no; they would not.
> *Kent:* Yes, they have.
> *Lear:* By Jupiter, I swear, no.
> *Kent:* By Juno, I swear, ay.
> *Lear:* They durst not do't;
> They could not, would not do't; 'tis worse than murder.

That iteration comes in with tremendous effect in Cassius' speech, made by all the recalcitrants of all ages about all the dictators, good or bad, of all ages:

> Brutus and Cæsar: what should be in that
>   ' Cæsar ' ?
> Why should that name be sounded more than
>   yours ?
> Write them together, yours is as fair a name;
> Sound them, it doth become the mouth as well;
> Weigh them, it is as heavy; conjure with 'em,
> ' Brutus ' will start a spirit as soon as ' Cæsar.'

The truth is, though, that it wouldn't. O rhetorical idealism, how many crimes are committed in thy name!

In *Richard III*, IV. 4, there is a long passage of antiphonal single lines in the best Greek manner. Brevity, when that was desirable, was the soul of his wit both in phrase and in speech. What eloquent romantic period could equal the first confession of the love-struck Juliet?

If he be married
My grave is like to be my wedding-bed.

" This is I, Hamlet the Dane," cries the Prince as he leaps into the grave; in *Troilus and Cressida*, V. 2, the few ejaculations of the watching Troilus contain enough matter for a chapter of a novel, an astonishing revelation of a state of mind under a succession of impacts; no profuse utterance could have contained more than Desdemona's pathetic: " I am very sorry that you are not well." The typical compactness of phrase that is manifested in a myriad of such summarizing sentences as Benedick's " Shall I never see a bachelor of three-score again? " and Volumnia's fiercely contemptuous " True! pow, wow! " and Cleopatra's (on first hearing of Antony's marriage) " I am pale " and Menenius's " Rome and her rats are at the point of battle " may be referred to in another chapter; here we are observing the economy of passages. What could be more hurried, more boding, more nocturnal, than the first sentences exchanged in *Julius*

Cæsar when Cinna encounters the conspirators Casca and Cassius in the dark street, under the sky disturbed by thunder and lightning?

> *Casca:* Stand close awhile, for here comes one in haste.
> *Cassius:* 'Tis Cinna; I do know him by his gait:
> He is a friend.
> (*Enter Cinna.*)
> Cinna, where haste you so?
> *Cinna:* To find out you. Who's that? Metellus Cimber?
> *Cassius:* No, it is Casca; one incorporate
> To our attempts. Am I not stay'd for, Cinna?
> *Cinna:* I am glad on't. What a fearful night is this! . . .
> *Cassius:* Am I not stay'd for? Tell me.

The first scene of all in the First Folio, the opening of *The Tempest*, strikes the note: in a few hasty exclamations, uttered on the deck of a storm-driven ship, a situation is indicated, characters and human relations suggested, a physical scene painted; and, in this masterpiece of expression, every sentence seems to flow in natural sequence, or natural inconsequence, from the last. That, again, is a distinguishing mark of Shakespeare's dialogue, as it must be of all good dialogue. A common defect of bad plays, particularly of bad plays by men-of-letters, is a failure to make the speeches of the characters evolve naturally: in ' poetic dramas ' the characters often seem to be much too much engaged upon making their own speeches to take much notice of other people, and connections, if established, are established artificially. In Shakespeare's plays, mind acts on mind, an idea arouses an idea, or a word provokes, by natural process, a word. His characters are fully aware of each other, they are ' with ' each other, they are affected by the emotions of others, they take cues from the inadvertent disclosures of others, they echo the melodies of others, they pursue others from point to point. The slow-witted grope after others' meanings, the quick-witted seize and twist others' words. His plays are scattered with life-like repartees, and the swift spontaneous distortions of humour. They have the force and crudity of life:

> *Beatrice:* I had rather hear my dog bark at a crow than a man swear he loves me.
> *Benedick:* God keep your ladyship still in that mind, so some gentleman or other shall 'scape a predestinate scratched face.
> *Beatrice:* Scratching could not make it worse, an 'twere such a face as yours were.

As good an instance is Patroclus' egging on of Thersites to ' rail '—excellently prepared for, by the way, in a previous indication of their pursuits. The debate in *Troilus and Cressida* is a real debate, with play of character and contention: though Hector, bravest and most pacific of them all, is perhaps too easily swayed at the end, the story needing it. Argument in Shakespeare influences people at least as frequently as it does in life, and convincingly: as when Catherine, after Wolsey's death, is persuaded by Griffith's eloquence at last to do justice to her enemy's great qualities. The excellence of his quarrels is symptomatic, whether the half-serious quarrels of not-yet-surrendered lovers or such quarrels as that, so full of fine feeling, so rapid in the flux of its passion, which overtook the self-contained **Brutus** and the lean neurotic Cassius when the shadow of death's wings was already over them. How they speak and answer, speak and **answer!**

> *Cassius:* **You wrong me every way; you wrong me, Brutus;**
> I said an elder soldier, not a better:
> Did I say ' better ' ?
> *Brutus:* **If you did, I care not.**
> *Cassius:* **When Cæsar liv'd, he durst not thus have mov'd me.**
> *Brutus:* **Peace, peace! you durst not so have tempted him.**
> *Cassius:* **I durst not!**
> *Brutus:* **No.**
> *Cassius:* **What! durst not tempt him!**
> *Brutus:* **For your life you durst not.**
> *Cassius:* **Do not presume too much upon my love;**
> I may do that I shall be sorry for.
> *Brutus:* **You have done that you should be sorry for.**

And for sheer naturalness both of phrase and of sequence no better instance may be given than the conversation between Hamlet and the officers who first report the ghost to him:

>*Hamlet:*   'Tis very strange.
>*Horatio:* As I do live, my honour'd lord, 'tis true;
>And we did think it writ down in our duty
>To let you know of it.
>*Hamlet:* Indeed, indeed, sirs, but this troubles me.
>Hold you the watch to-night?
>*Mar. Ber.:*   We do, my lord.
>*Hamlet:* Arm'd, say you?
>*Mar. Ber.:*   Arm'd, my lord.
>*Hamlet:*   From top to toe?
>*Mar. Ber.:* My lord, from head to foot.
>*Hamlet:* Then saw you not his face?
>*Horatio:* O yes! my lord; he wore his beaver up.
>*Hamlet:* What! look'd he frowningly?
>*Horatio:* A countenance more in sorrow than in anger.
>*Hamlet:* Pale or red?
>*Horatio:* Nay, very pale.
>*Hamlet:*   And fix'd his eyes upon you?
>*Horatio:* Most constantly.
>*Hamlet:*   I would I had been there.
>*Horatio:* It would have much amazed you.
>*Hamlet:* Very like, very like. Stay'd it long?
>*Horatio:* While one with moderate haste might tell a hundred.
>*Mar. Ber.:* Longer, longer.
>*Horatio:* Not when I saw it.
>*Hamlet:*   His beard was grizzled, no?

Horatio: It was, as I have seen it in his life,
A sable silver'd.
Hamlet: I will watch to-night;
Perchance 'twill walk again.

Such a passage—not the supreme effort of a climax, but mere preparation for a plot—is enough to drive any later essayist in dialogue to despair. A book might be written on all the merits of it. With what miraculous firmness are the character and the unspoken thoughts of Hamlet indicated in every sentence he utters! How he fastens on the significant things, and half-hears, whilst his own mind feverishly works, the others! How inevitable is the sequence of his questions; how pregnant even that brief interrogation " No ? " and his abstracted " Very like, very like "! How clear all the stages that lead up to his resolution to watch! How characteristic is Hamlet's " top to toe " contrasted with the more conventional phrase of the soldiers! We seem to hear the sound of each voice, speaking as it must; did either Marcellus or Bernardo leave the other to speak alone any of their three sentences in union, we should notice something wrong! And it must be remembered that he was working without scenery. As Mr. Granville-Barker says:

When we learn with a shock of surprise—having begun in the schoolroom upon the Shakespeare of the editors, it comes as belated news to us—that neither battlements, throne-rooms, nor picturesque churchyards were to be seen at the Globe, and that " Elsinore, a platform before the Castle " is not

Shakespeare at all, we yet imagine ourselves among the audience there busily conjuring these things up with the eye of faith. He had to do with words what we now do, less adequately, with paint.

Here, as in the later scene on the platform, as again in the second-act passage with Rosencrantz and Guildenstern, we are in the presence of dialogue dramatic in the fullest sense: doing every kind of work that dialogue can do, at a moment fraught with significance. The bones of the play are being articulated. Slack though Shakespeare may often be—or his actors, or his copiers, or his printers—in linking up passages, his genius for perfection never fails him when perfection is most needed. The greatest things he does most greatly, the most difficult with most apparent ease. Hysterical vilification and pleading; the coiling soliloquy, the fragmentary whisper, the flashing exchange, the sharp cessation of speech, dead silence; the utmost tones of joy, tenderness, horror, grief and despair: all strings of the harp he touches with sure fingers, all keys he commands, all spirits he summons from the deep, and they come. How immeasurably he intensifies the horror of the boy Arthur's situation, after we in the audience know that the irons have been heated red for him, when he makes him, innocently complaining but of tedious confinement, speak his childish wish so simply and naturally!

By my christendom,
So I were out of prison and kept sheep,

> I should be as merry as the day is long;
> And so I would be here, but that I doubt
> My uncle practises more harm to me.

That murderous, hypocritical uncle, whose own state of mind is shortly to be superbly indicated with the uneasy growl:

> Why do you bend such solemn brows on me?
> Think you I bear the shears of destiny?
> Have I commandment on the pulse of life?

A similar effect is made when Cleopatra, going in sad splendour to her death, calls back the past as she gives her last orders to her tiring-women:

> Now, Charmian!
> Show me, my women, like a queen; go fetch
> My best attires; I am again for Cydnus
> To meet Mark Antony.

It has the dramatic force of truth; in a less sombre context there is something akin to it in the young Arviragus's yearning out to a distant and larger world from his mountain fastness in *Cymbeline*:

> What should we speak of
> When we are as old as you? When we shall hear
> The rain and wind beat dark December, how
> In this our pinching cave shall we discourse
> The freezing hours away. We have seen nothing.

Shakespeare here, by a cunning use of his imagination, at once enforces belief in his whole fable and produces an atmosphere of expectancy. So, heightening a crucial action to come, did Shakespeare prepare for Juliet's death by her dreadful imaginative vision of a possible waking in the charnel-house: "the horrible conceit of death and night." Dialogue is his docile slave when he desires a dramatic change of tone, a swift crescendo of emotion, a momentous intentness, a storm, a burdened hush, like those in *Macbeth*, or that which falls when Leontes' little doomed son, Mamillius, so tragically intelligent and imaginative, eagerly draws the kindly condescending ladies round the fire with him, that he may begin his thrilling story: "There was a man . . . Dwelt by a churchyard," taking in, the while, the quick breaths of childish excitement. In his few words, this motherless child, so soon to die, discloses himself as a brave and gentle genius, nipped young in the bud. The body of words and the soul of dramatic movement are as one and indivisible in such passionate outbursts as the jealous Leontes' "Is whispering nothing? Is leaning cheek to cheek? Is meeting noses?" or Crookback's: "Out on ye, owls! nothing but songs of death!" or his great speech after his bloody dream. The crowned Hal's calm disclaimer of Falstaff, his former companion: "I know thee not, old man," is a masterpiece of dramatic compression; so also the discrowned Richard's "What more remains?" a phrase of utter surrender that makes him superior to all around him. And *Othello* is packed with such things:

> *Desdemona:* My lord, what is your will?
> *Othello:* Pray, chuck, come hither.
> *Desdemona:* What is your pleasure?
> *Othello:* Let me see your eyes; Look in my face.
> *Desdemona:* What horrible fancy's this?

So begins the scene that leads up to that terrible raving: the restraint, the dreadful, almost maniacal use of the affectionate " chuck," the feverish brevity and intensity. And here is illustrated also one more characteristic of Shakespeare: the certainty and clarity with which he indicates action. The physical gestures are determined by the very words that express the emotion.

The words of the waiters outside Aufidius' banquet-hall in *Coriolanus* rush and scramble like the waiters themselves; the banquet set and work suspended, more leisurely talk begins; to be suddenly interrupted at the end with: " They are rising, they are rising. In, in, in, in "—calculation having even determined the number of those " in's." " Silence that dreadful bell," cries Othello, and the whole scene is conjured up. " Look I so pale, Lord Dorset, as the rest? " asks Buckingham: we see him as well as the rest; " Good, very good; it is so then: good, very good. Let it be concealed awhile," exclaims Parolles after Lafeu has explored both his conceit and poltroonery, and every word implies a movement of face or limb. There is no need of the stage direction 'starting' when just at the moment that Richard is most sweating at the recollection of his dreadful nocturnal vision Ratcliff steps into the tent:

> *Ratcliff:* My lord!
> *Richard:* Zounds! who is there?

All that is necessary is given in those momentously laconic sentences when Cæsar goes up to the Senate House:

> *Popilius:* I wish your enterprise to-day may thrive.
> *Cassius:* What enterprise, Popilius?
> *Pop.:*   Fare you well.

And the repeated "Anon, sir" of Francis in *Henry IV*, Part I, Act II, Scene 4, both gives the scene briskness and indicates its place. All is clearly devised and clearly seen by Shakespeare; and his dialogue is drenched with his vision. There was with him, when he did not quite know what would happen, no question of saying: "We'll leave that to the producer"; and in an age which had little truck with elaborate scenery, and never dreamed of whole-page stage directions, or plays for the study, he left nothing to the ingenuity of the scene painter and the property-man. It might be argued that elaborate stage directions and expensive specified lighting and scenery relieve the dramatist's dialogue of a load of which it can well afford to be relieved. When another dramatist achieves Shakespeare's utterly convincing effects of reality, and proves that he has seen with Shakespeare's absolute vision, the argument may be given a hearing: the probability is that the limitations of the old stage were a discipline and a stimulus, not a burden or a handicap.

> *Second Murderer:* Look behind you, my lord.
> *First Murderer:* Take that, and that! (*stabs him*).

With an apparently effortless facility, in the natural course of conversation, Shakespeare habitually suggests action, immediate scene, a world beyond. We need not be told that we are in a garden before a house (2 *Henry IV*, V. 3) when Shallow and Falstaff, entering, begin:

> *Shallow:* Nay, you shall see mine orchard, where, in an arbour, we will eat a last year's pippin of my own graffing, with a dish of caraways, and so forth; come, cousin Silence; and then to bed.
> *Falstaff:* 'Fore God, you have here a goodly dwelling and a rich.

The whole country scene is immediately presented to us: not to mention the meal from which they have obviously just come, the even rustic life of Shallow, the ancient acquaintance of the pair, now so different in habit and fortune, the sloping away, from youth on, of their characters, the half-envy that the wilful, rootless old knight feels when he contemplates the prosperity of an old acquaintance, not a tithe as intelligent or experienced as himself.

> *Cæsar:* Welcome to Rome.
> *Antony:* Thank you.
> *Cæsar:* Sit.
> *Antony:* Sit, sir.
> *Cæsar:* Nay, then.

That little passage saves a world of stage directions, besides adding to the verisimilitude of what comes after. " The King is angry: see, he gnaws his lip," from Catesby, is an aside and a clumsier substitute. But consider this:

> *Macbeth:* The table's full.
> *Lennox:* Here is a place reserv'd, sir.
> *Macbeth:* Where?
> *Lennox:* Here, my good lord. What is't that moves your highness?
> *Macbeth:* Which of you have done this?
> *Lords:* What, my good lord?
> *Macbeth:* Thou canst not say I did it: never shake
> Thy gory locks at me.
> *Ross:* Gentlemen, rise; his highness is not well.
> *Lady Mac.:* Sit, worthy friends: my lord is often thus.

Thunderous with dramatic force: yet much briefer than the stage directions which, with so much else, it comprehends, and which, infallibly, a modern dramatist would have chosen to set down, as it were, first, in that very action determining that his dialogue should be less vital than it need be. And once, after a splendid tempest has ended, he uses the concrete 'stage-direction' element in his dialogue to intensify his pathos at the very end of the play:

> *First Guard:*   O Cæsar!
> This Charmian liv'd but now; she stood, and
>   spake:
> I found her trimming up the diadem
> On her dead mistress; tremblingly she stood
> And on the sudden dropp'd.

Cæsar, we know from his words, stands apart, thinking not of Charmian, but of the Queen dead before him. Dolabella kneels over the body.

> *Dolabella:*   Here, on her breast,
> There is a vent of blood, and something blown;
> The like is on her arm.
>   *First Guard:* This is an aspic's trail; and these
>   fig-leaves
> Have slime upon them, such as the aspic leaves
> Upon the caves of Nile.

The two "leaves" suggest an imperfect text: otherwise how perfect.

CHAPTER VII
DIALOGUE: MINOR DEVICES

In dialogue which did not strictly spring from the situation or forward the plot Shakespeare resorted to every conceivable device for amusing or incidentally interesting the audience. Coleridge said that Shakespeare never "wrote down": if so "the less Shakespeare he." Certainly a dramatist is a "base mechanical" if he abandons his own view of life to suit an audience, or forces his conclusions to comfort them: but in matters of detail it is his business to entertain them as thoroughly as he can, always provided that he does not impair his main effects in the effort to secure subsidiary ones.

Shakespeare frequently made use of the topical or local allusion to excite applause or raise a laugh. Some of his references to great events and personages, Essex, Leicester and the Queen—"the fair vestal thronèd in the west"—are obvious: many more have been conjectured. He was content to fly at much smaller game than that. References in the theatre to the theatre are always piquant. He was free with them. Such a reference as that in *Romeo and Juliet* to a

without-book prologue, faintly spoke
After the prompter

would have made a special hit on days when the Prologue to this very play (possibly acting under instructions) falteringly followed the prompts. There is a topical appeal, mingled with the rest, in much of Hamlet's advice to the players. The whole audience must have thought of particular ranters when Hamlet implored the actors to leave off strutting and bellowing, as did those Thespians who " neither having the accents of Christians nor the gait of Christian, pagan or man " were nevertheless by some praised " and that highly." And the legs of the Tarletons and Kempes all would realize were being pulled when he added: " And let those that play your clowns speak no more than is set down for them; for there be some of them that will themselves laugh, to set on some quantity of barren spectators to laugh too, though in the meantime some necessary question of the play be then to be considered "—at which the audience must laugh at themselves. Another local theatrical reference in this play is that to the " aery of children " competing with the common players and being " most tyrannically clapped for it." And in an age when all women's parts were taken by male children the audience must have been poignantly moved (if they were not amused) by Cleopatra's dread of being represented on the stage by " a squeaking boy." How cunning it was boldly to admit that play and audience were in the theatre in order to persuade the audience that it was not!

The perpetual ward-constable in *Measure for Measure* who takes on other men's civic duties for pay must have been a familiar figure to Elizabethan audiences; the facetious reference in *All's Well* to the man who had " beaten the drum before the tragedies " and been " an officer at a place there called Mile-End to instruct for the doubling of files" will have raised a laugh against the trained bands; and the religious ardours of the moment were strongly appealed to by King John when he appended to his statement of revolt against Rome an allusion to " vile gold, dross, dust " which

> Purchase corrupted pardon of a man
> Who in that sale sells pardon from himself.

Jokes about the English on the lips of foreigners were popular then as now. In *Henry V* (which is also full of comic foreigners, French, Irish, Welsh) the Constable says, on the eve of Agincourt, of the English: " Give them great meals of beef and iron and steel, they will eat like wolves and fight like devils." In *Hamlet* there is this dialogue:

> *First Clo.:* It was the very day that young Hamlet was born; he that is mad, and sent into England.
> *Hamlet:* Ay, marry; why was he sent into England ?
> *First Clo.:* Why, because he was mad: he shall recover his wits there; or, if he do not, 'tis no great matter there.
> *Hamlet:* Why ?
> *First Clo.:* 'Twill not be seen in him there; there the men are mad as he.

Englishmen still find delight and satisfaction in the thought that all foreigners think them mad. This jest holds; so also the more important and bitterer one in:

> That one may smile, and smile, and be a villain;
> At least I'm sure it may be so in Denmark.

And we can at least understand how strong, to an Elizabethan audience, used to the heroes and doubtless the pseudo-heroes of Flanders and the Spanish Main, would have been the appeal of Gower's observations in *Henry V*, vivid with contemporary manners:

> Why, 'tis a gull, a fool, a rogue, that now and then goes to the wars to grace himself at his return into London under the form of a soldier. And such fellows are perfect in the great commanders' names, and they will learn you by rote where services were done; at such and such a sconce, at such a breach, at such a convoy; who came off bravely, who was shot, who disgraced, what terms the enemy stood on; and this they con perfectly in the phrase of war, which they trick up with new-tuned oaths; and what a beard of the general's cut and a horrid suit of the camp will do among foaming bottles and ale-washed wits, is wonderful to be thought on.

Many of Shakespeare's remarks, particularly those addressed to the knowledge or prejudices of his audience about the fashions of speech and dress of the day, are now flat or incomprehensible to us. Scholars may annotate them and restore part of their force: music and general truth alone certainly abide.

He used the topical allusion to politics and manners; he used also the topical allusion to literature. He parodied the styles of authors, and he parodied the styles of characters on the stage itself. Thus Dogberry is burlesqued; whilst Hamlet parodies the obscure verbosity of Osric to the guileless Osric's face, and then, at the highest pitch of excitement, echoes Laertes' bombast at him, breathlessly ending: " Nay, an thou'lt mouth, I'll rant as well as thou." The airy direction at the beginning of *Pericles*:

SCENE: Dispersedly in various countries.

we cannot hope, alas! to be a reflection on an unstable tendency of the day. Some of the verse rehearsed by the Players in the second Act of *Hamlet*, and some of that spoken by them in the third Act, is just too good to be diagnosed as mere burlesque: all that Shakespeare was trying to do, probably, was to differentiate the style from his own, and anything different was bound to be inferior. There is, however, no doubt at all about his hilarious assaults on the two vilest and most flourishing literary fashions of his day: Euphuism and melodramatic Bombast. A delicious travesty of Lyly's absurd antithesis is put in the deliciously incongruous mouth of Sir John Falstaff:

> For though the camomile, the more it is trodden on the faster it grows, yet youth, the more it is wasted the sooner it wears

—which he follows up with his admirably pedantic remark,

> This pitch, as ancient writers do report, doth defile

—which might almost have come out of *The Anatomy of Melancholy*. And the corrupt issue of the most magniloquent, and sufficiently bad, passages in Marlowe and Kyd are beautifully travestied in the speeches of Pistol:

> Shall dunghill curs confront the Helicons?
> And shall good news be baffled?
> Then Pistol, lay thy head in Furies' lap.
>
> Under which king, Bezonian? speak or die!
>
> Let vultures vile seize on his lungs also!
>
> My knight I will inflame thy noble liver,
> And make thee rage.
> Thy Doll, and Helen of thy noble thoughts
> Is in base durance and contagious prison;
> Hal'd thither
> By most mechanical and dirty hand:
> Rouse up revenge from ebon den with fell
>   Alecto's snake,
> For Doll is in: Pistol speaks nought but truth.

Parts of this are utterly meaningless. Sheer gibberish, discreetly employed, and uttered by a suitable person, with the right accent of confidence, innocence or slyness, is always effective in the theatre. Shakespeare was sparing with it. The Clown in *Twelfth Night*, with his " I did impeticos thy gratillity," has his share, but the most effective use of it is in *All's Well that Ends Well*, where the French Lord and soldiers punish the cowardly braggart Parolles by pretending that they are foreign soldiers who have captured him, and speaking " chough's language, gabble enough and good enough " :

> *First Lord:* Throca movousus, cargo, cargo, cargo.
> *All:* Cargo, cargo, villianda par corbo, cargo.
>   (*They seize and blindfold him.*)
> *Par.:* O! ransom, ransom! Do not hide mine eyes.
> *First Sold.:* Boskos thromuldo boskos.
> *Par.:* I know you are the Muskos' regiment;
> And I shall lose my life for want of language.
> If there be here German or Dane, Low Dutch,
> Italian or French, let him speak to me:
> I will discover that which shall undo
> The Florentine.
> *First Sold.:*   Boskos vauvado:
> I understand thee and can speak thy tongue:
> *Kerelybonto:* Sir,
> Betake thee to thy faith, for seventeen poniards
> Are at thy bosom.
>   *Par.:*   O!
>   *First Sold.:*   O! pray, pray, pray.
> Manka revania dulche.
>   *First Lord:*   Oscorbidulchos volivorco.

The situation is comic enough in all conscience: so also Parolles' catalogue of the languages he knows and the sentence about the seventeen poniards, far though this may fall short of Gibbon's extreme hyperbole: " A thousand swords were plunged at once into the bosom of the unfortunate Probus." Yet in the theatre the loudest laughs will be roused by the gibberish, valued for its own sweet sake—no condescension, perhaps, on the part of a Shakespeare who shared the delights of the vulgar, but surely enough to raise doubts in the breast of a Coleridge.

The malapropism is an allied device, and akin also to the comic English talked by foreigners, French, Welsh, Irish—Caius, Evans, Kate, Fluellen —of which Shakespeare, like ten thousand of his successors, made good use. It is a sure success with the unsophisticated and natural, but now " fallen on evil days and evil tongues " in suburban and provincial pantomimes, where a man who calls a twoshilling piece a " pea-shilling tooce " or lets slip something about the " immorality of the soul " can still count on his triumph, with the eponymous heroine of the genre, and Dogberry. Pompey and Elbow have a small display in *Measure for Measure*, and the Host in *Two Gentlemen* speaks of an " allycholly " disposition; but with Dogberry Shakespeare exploits the malapropism without reserve. " Comparisons are odorous," is Dogberry's: a phrase in which the nascent humour of every schoolboy has delighted, though he knows not its source:

"Flat burglary as ever was committed," he exclaims after he has "comprehended two aspicious persons," and "O villain, thou wilt be condemned into everlasting redemption for this." His also is: "It will be suffigance," in which he anticipated the very manner of Mrs. Gamp and her "so dispoged." The device of giving a man a catch-phrase which he repeats in all manner of suitable and unsuitable occasions was also employed by Shakespeare. He found in *Henry V* that Corporal Nym's gag, "And that's the humour of it," always produced laughter; so he exploited it thoroughly in the *Merry Wives*, where Nym's 'humours' occur no fewer than five times in one short speech. Nobody can call that realism or say that it was necessary for characterization: it is there because Shakespeare knew it would 'fetch' an audience—an excellent reason—and he aimed at the audience precisely as he did with such adaptations of words as Stephano's about Caliban: "This is a devil and no monster: I will leave him: I have no long spoon." And always, occasion serving, he gave his groundlings full measure of that Billingsgate vituperation, the torrential flow of which, from angry man, habitual railer, or (best still) virago always delights an audience *per se* and irrespective of its surroundings. Thersites' is a whole part of railing: there are plenty of passages like that denunciation of Oswald by Kent, a pyramid of obloquy culminating in: "And art nothing but the composition of a knave, beggar, coward, pandar, and the son and heir of a mongrel bitch."

All excessive speech, the abandonment of abuse, of comic self-concern, or of bombast was at Shakespeare's finger-ends, and he flung specimens of it at the general whenever they might be tired of caviare —granted always that he never, or scarcely ever, did it unworthily, with deleterious results to his main theme. In his own day it is likely that there was a laugh at a very inappropriate moment in *Othello*, IV. 3, where Othello says to Desdemona: " I have a pain upon my forehead here "—we can only hope that Shakespeare's puckishness was not really at work here. In a general way his instinct is certainly unerring: he never lets us down in his big scenes. In the intervals he will say anything to amuse.

> These lily lips,
> This cherry nose,
> These yellow cowslip cheeks

always gets the guffaws, but is scarcely the cream of Shakespeare's humour, nor did he think it so. And this repartee of Falstaff's, one feels, must have been suggested by some buffoon actors at rehearsal:

Chief Justice: There is not a white hair upon your face but should have his effect of gravity.
Falstaff: His effect of gravy, gravy, gravy.

With the fatuous word play about " mollis aer " and " mulier " in *Cymbeline* we will not saddle him: it probably made his spine as cold as it makes ours. But the citizens presumably laughed when the Fool

in *Lear* made his pun on " dolours " and " dollars ";
and there is the very smack of circus drollery in his
" 'Twas her brother that, in pure kindness to his
horse, buttered the hay." Even with the " dolours "
before me I can only half believe that the line in
Romeo and Juliet:

> Flies may do this, but I from this must fly

is by Shakespeare. It is of unsurpassed silliness, un-
gainliness and ineffectiveness; however low Shakespeare, at however early an age, may have sunk to
tickle the groundlings, can he really have abased
himself thus to produce a line at which not even the
groundlings could laugh, and at a moment when the
very groundlings might resent even the best of puns?
A similar appeal is made by the slapstick episode in
The Taming of the Shrew:

> *Grumio:* Thereby hangs a tale.
> *Curtis:* Let's ha't, good Grumio.
> *Grumio:* Lend thine ear.
> *Curtis:* Here.
> *Grumio*: There.   (*Striking him.*)
> *Curtis:* This is to feel a tale, not to hear a tale.

This may hold the mirror up to a certain part of
nature; but it is of the world of Joey, Father and
the Policeman. A like farcical effect is elsewhere
achieved by Asides, which could have been avoided
so far as their mere conveyance of information is
concerned: notably the very effective string shot at
the audience by the Second Lord while his companion is talking to Cloten in *Cymbeline*, I. 2.

CHAPTER VIII

DIALOGUE: SOLILOQUIES AND LONG SPEECHES

SOME very interesting and important questions arise when one contemplates Shakespeare's use and abuse of long speeches, and, in particular, long soliloquies. Except that, according to the modern convention, soliloquies are now regarded as unpardonable deformities in construction and stratagems not to be used, there is no clean line of division between a speech made by a man with other characters on the stage and a speech that he makes *solus*: remarks which are, superficially, addressed to other characters may be in effect soliloquies if they make no impression on them and are intended to elicit no response. The long address and the long soliloquy are plentiful in Shakespeare: they were a fashion not outgrown—at any rate not discarded—in his day, the day (be it remembered) of the apron platform, when the actor had a more familiar relation with the audience than he can have on his modern removed stage. At all events, the long soliloquy was part of the young English drama. Shakespeare, also, was a poet with an infinite flow of idea and fancy, and had a natural tendency, once started on an oratorical or descriptive flight, to go on.

Shakespeare's long speeches may be divided roughly into two classes. There are those which

DIALOGUE : SOLILOQUIES AND LONG SPEECHES 207

are part of the dramatic movement, or the natural product of the action of situation and character: and there are those which are not, but are essentially interpolations 'holding up' the play. These last may again be divided into speeches which we nevertheless accept with delight in the theatre and speeches which we do not. The soliloquy qua soliloquy need not be discussed here. It is certainly an expedient fraught with dreadful dangers to idle or incompetent dramatists, who load upon it work they are unable or unwilling to do in what in our day, though not in Shakespeare's, is a less abnormal and more convincing way. The present reaction against it is attributable to its grave abuse: there are limits to what a man can convincingly be made to think aloud, to talk about to himself. But, inherently, it is no more inexpedient than any other mode of communication. It is arbitrary to ask us to believe in long speeches made by a character alone; but all the other ingredients in a play are equally artificial and all the other assumptions we accept equally arbitrary. There is one, and only one, test which can properly be applied to this or any other tool of the dramatic technician: that is, the extent to which it 'holds' an audience and contributes towards the general effect aimed at. This general question must be passed over: and there is another which is tempting but must be ignored. That is the extent to which the admissibility of long speeches, and especially long undramatic speeches, varies according to the play in which they are introduced. Surroundings make a difference. When swift action is expected, a long interruption and suspense may be ruinous; in such a play as Fletcher's Arcadian Pastoral, *The Faithful Shepherdess*, which aims much more at producing an atmosphere than at presenting a sequence of events, we do not mind how long we are detained by pretty ruminations and descriptions; it all helps the scenery. What in one place is but an unnecessary pretty word becomes in another a disastrous piece of procrastination, fatally destructive to illusion.

Some of Shakespeare's longest soliloquies and speeches in dialogue—which is to say some of his noblest passages of sustained poetry—are as perfectly dramatic as they are beautifully thought, felt and phrased. Malvolio's soliloquies—all the richer when we see that they are overheard—are close woven with the texture of the play's development: we hang upon every word for revelation. Lear's long ravings are all to the point, the spontaneous cries of a proud heart, moved by agony and a powerful intellect, broken by intolerable distress, passionately and tempestuously releasing the suppressed observations and reflections of a life now, at its close, newly orientated towards the cold constellations of despair. Othello's declamations are superb. They are speech as well as speeches, even the long necessary narrative (but how sweet a scene that would have been to possess directly) of how young Desdemona's love was won by his stories of

DIALOGUE : SOLILOQUIES AND LONG SPEECHES

far wonders and great deeds. The last of them is marvellously right in its place, the valediction of this great soul still kept noble by a manly pride, borne by the very magnitude, the utter irreparability, of his disaster, into a place of awful peace on the farther side of Remorse:

> *Othello:* Soft you; a word or two before you go.
> I have done the state some service, and they know't;
> No more of that. I pray you, in your letters,
> When you shall these unlucky deeds relate,
> Speak of me as I am; nothing extenuate,
> Nor set down aught in malice.

The phrase:

> Drop tears as fast as the Arabian trees
> Their med'cinable gum

is inappropriate on such lips at such a moment; too composed, though of sweet tune and fragrance. Did Shakespeare keep it here because its music too had a touch of the "med'cinable"? In *The Merchant of Venice*, I. 1, Shylock has, first of all, a soliloquy ("How like a fawning publican he looks!") which bears strictly upon the situation, and then makes a long speech ("Signor Antonio, many a time and oft") which is intensely concentrated upon the situation. Not a word is *dramatically* superfluous, even the 'favourite quotation' (for many of the favourite quotations in Shakespeare come from his least dramatic passages): "For sufferance is the badge of all our tribe." Elsewhere, in this play, there are speeches of which as much cannot be said. In certain of Hamlet's soliloquies Shakespeare conveys a great deal of information as to the progress of his intentions and the nature of his complicated hesitations. Here (though the speeches are padded out with superfluous marvels) the play is naturally, and seems inevitably, helped on by the soliloquies: there is much that Hamlet could communicate to no one, and nothing that the audience must feel entitled to have seen shown to them in specific scene and conversation. Henry V's Hamlet-like soliloquy on the eve of Agincourt, lovely to read, rather long for the stage, may also be dramatically defended in part: it arises out of his talk with the soldiers, a solitary vigil by the responsible person, while the others sleep, is natural, and the thoughts are in substance such as might occur to him, though portions of it sound rather like Shakespeare than Henry, and we tend to smile (considering the situation) when this particular King complains that the public do not realize "what watch the King keeps to maintain the peace." But in a soliloquy of Iago's, dramatic use is certainly made of the method, but in a manner more difficult for us to feel natural. In *Othello*, II. 3, that villain, on a cleared stage, speaks thus:

> If I can fasten but one cup upon him,
> With that which he hath drunk to-night already,
> He'll be as full of quarrel and offence

DIALOGUE : SOLILOQUIES AND LONG SPEECHES 211

    As my young mistress' dog. Now, my sick
      fool, Roderigo,
    Whom love has turn'd almost the wrong side
      out,
    To Desdemona hath to-night carous'd
    Potations pottle deep; and he's to watch.
    Three lads of Cyprus, noble swelling spirits,
    That hold their honours in a wary distance,
    The very elements of this war-like isle
    Have I to-night fluster'd with flowing cups,
    And they watch too. Now, 'mongst this flock
      of drunkards,
    Am I to put our Cassio in some action
    That may offend the isle. But here they come:
    If consequence do but approve my dream,
    My boat sails freely, both with wind and stream.

Now, this is not there as a piece of self-communing, inner argument or reverie, which a man might plausibly murmur aloud when pacing up and down by himself, or might exclaim aloud at a moment of excitement: though the last lines might reasonably pass as such. It is simply " telling the audience," telling them what has happened to other people, what is going to happen, what he himself plots to do: things which, if necessary to the development and understanding of the plot, should have been shown or indicated in ordinary stage dialogue and action: it is an easy summary, an indolent evasion: it is even to some extent an unnecessary anticipation which lowers excitement when the event comes. Iago has a habit of explanation by soliloquy, and most of his solitary speeches we accept. But this one, which could so easily have been spoken to a confederate, were Iago capable of one, must seem awkward to any modern audience, even if it realizes that he is declaring himself puppet-master.

All these passages, strong or weak, are 'doing something'—legitimately or not legitimately, well or badly. There are many such which do less or little or nothing from the strictly dramatic point of view. These include some of the loveliest and some of the most majestic speeches in Shakespeare.

We will (before a last word on the rights of the matter) consider a few, chosen out of multitudes, which would have been either compressed or eliminated by any competent modern dramatist; or if not by him, then by his manager or producer. One of the most signal specimens is Mercutio's exquisite account of Queen Mab and her equipage, which contains the quintessence of all the fairy poetry in the *Dream* and Drayton's *Nymphidia*. In the same play Romeo's last speech, a strange mixture of dramatic dialogue and padding, exquisite poetry and cold tropes (such as the legal " a dateless bargain to engrossing death) would be very much more effective intrinsically, and expedite the expected end, were it cut. Take, again, Orlando's speech when he first encounters the Duke and his cultivated outlaws in *As You Like It*:

> *Orlando:* Speak you so gently? Pardon me, I pray you:
> I thought that all things had been savage here,
> And therefore put I on the countenance

> Of stern commandment. But whate'er you are
> That in this desert inaccessible,
> Under the shade of melancholy boughs,
> Lose and neglect the creeping hours of time;
> If ever you have look'd on better days,
> If ever been where bells have knoll'd to church,
> If ever sat at any good man's feast,
> If ever from your eyelids wip'd a tear,
> And know what 'tis to pity, and be pitied,
> Let gentleness my strong enforcement be:
> In the which hope I blush, and hide my sword.

To which the Duke, in tautologous antiphony, replies:

> *Duke:* True is it that we have seen better days,
> And have with holy bell been knoll'd to church,
> And sat at good men's feasts, and wip'd our eyes
> Of drops that sacred pity hath engender'd.

The laconic modern school, which has reached the point of preferring silence to speech if silence can be made eloquent, would scarcely need more for that first utterance than: " Forgive me. I thought that there could be nothing but savages in such a place. I am almost done "—or " done in." A few lines later comes Jaques' speech on the Seven Ages of Man; " All the world's a stage." It is one of the most marvellous things in literature, a conspectus of life, a mosaic of miraculous epithet and phrase. It perfunctorily arises from the Duke's last remarks about " the wide and universal theatre "; but its lack of organic connection with the play is evident, and would be glaringly more so were the amazing phraseology of Shakespeare's remarks scrapped and a more banal expression of them substituted. It adds nothing, assists nothing, provokes nothing; it is not here even useful for the mere disconnected characterization of Jaques. Jaques might have said it all at any other time; he might even have said it with more excuse had " a lean and slippered pantaloon " been presented to him to make his thought more nearly inevitable. The play is arrested while he delivers the declamation; the play as a drama would be precisely what it is were the declamation excised. Or take again the Queen's description of Ophelia's death. This speech is in another category, because it was natural and fitting that somebody should announce the essential facts that it discloses. But consider the manner, the amplitude, the ornamental amplitude, of the speech as it stands in *Hamlet*:

> There is a willow grows aslant a brook,
> That shows his hoar leaves in the glassy stream;
> There with fantastic garlands did she come,
> Of crow-flowers, nettles, daisies, and long purples,
> That liberal shepherds give a grosser name,
> But our cold maids do dead men's fingers call them:
> There, on the pendent boughs her coronet weeds
> Clambering to hang, an envious sliver broke,
> When down her weedy trophies and herself

>   Fell in the weeping brook.   Her clothes spread
>   wide,
> And, mermaid-like, awhile they bore her up;
> Which time she chanted snatches of old tunes,
> As one incapable of her own distress,
> Or like a creature native and indu'd
> Unto that element; but long it could not be
> Till that her garments, heavy with their drink,
> Pull'd the poor wretch from her melodious lay
> To muddy death.

Judged by any dramatic conventions except the Elizabethan,[1] what is there to be said for this? "That liberal shepherds give a grosser name," indeed! What has that to do with it, and how could the Queen, at such a moment of emotion, concern herself with this glossary of botanic nomenclature? Twenty words are used where one would 'do the work': no attempt is made to give the Queen's individual reactions; she does not speak in character but, for the moment, becomes the mere mouthpiece of the most mellifluous of poets; instead of a dramatic messenger of death or a horrified mother we have a tender and careful Pre-Raphaelite painter of willows and water, a maid distraught, and peaceful death among the flowers. Shakespeare, presumably by deliberation, places it where it would

---

[1] Rowe smelt a rat when he said: " If one undertook to examine the greatest part of these by those rules which were establish'd by Aristotle, and taken from the model of the Grecian Stage, it would be no hard task to find a great many Faults: but as Shakespear liv'd under a kind of mere Light of Nature, and had never been acquainted with the Regularity of those written Precepts, so it would be hard to judge him by a Law he knew nothing of."

(even were nothing else to be said for it) do one service: at the close of an exciting scene, and immediately before a scene which opens with the rich, terse, grim, thrilling dialogue of the grave-diggers: " Is she to be buried in Christian burial, that wilfully seeks her own salvation?" The fact remains that this is not dramatic speech, in the normal sense, but written much as Shakespeare must have written it had he composed a descriptive narrative, *Hamlet and Ophelia*, on the lines of Marlowe's *Hero and Leander*. The very order is dramatically all wrong. Imagine running in to say that a girl has just been drowned and leisurely observing: " There is a willow grows aslant a brook"!

Yet most of these passages of wise rumination, sentimental reminiscence, lovely description, we not only would on no account lose from the plays as reading, but would not consent to forgo in the theatre. Shakespeare is all scattered with lovely passages that are not strictly dramatic, passages incidental or irrelevant which he manages to " get away with " in the theatre. Our modern views about play-making are a thought too rigid. If we are held by a detail, and the detail does not impair a major effect, the detail is justified. There is no *a priori* reason why, provided a dramatist can bring off these difficult coups, recitations should not be interpolated in a play as much as dances. There is poetry, and there is drama and there is poetic drama. Granted a lovely enough description, we can even, in Shakespeare, be content to allow an important thing to happen off-stage. People who complain of Shakespeare's more vagrant soliloquies and speeches do not complain of his songs, which are a still more detached medium for 'secreting' the superabundant wealth of his poetry. Who would surrender that loveliest of all speeches, Perdita's before the shepherd's cottage:

> Now, my fair'st friend,
> I would I had some flowers o' the spring that might
> Become your time of day; and yours, and yours,
> That wear upon your virgin branches yet
> Your maidenheads growing: O Proserpina!
> For the flowers now that frighted thou let'st fall
> From Dis's waggon! daffodils,
> That come before the swallow dares, and take
> The winds of March with beauty; violets dim,
> But sweeter than the lids of Juno's eyes
> Or Cytherea's breath; pale prime-roses,
> That die unmarried, ere they can behold
> Bright Phœbus in his strength, a malady
> Most incident to maids; bold oxlips and
> The crown imperial; lilies of all kinds,
> The flower-de-luce being one.

Parts of this catalogue may have some reference to the company, and her mere making of it does give us some light upon the depth and sweetness of Perdita; but primarily, in the theatre, it is the most exquisite of recitations. It is so exquisite that we care not how long it shall go on, so that the images be of that auroral softness and clarity, the music of flow and pause, of vowel-sequence, assonance and alliteration, as ravishing, as chastely voluptuous, as tenderly restrained: and when it ends, the heart in us cries like Faust, " Stay, fleeting moment, stay," for we would have the voice of Perdita go on for ever, falling on our troubles like dew, and soothing us into a felicity of oblivion to all except the blissful pain of beauty, pure, perfect and intangible as the rainbow's, that arches the sky in momentary glory, and wanes against a cloud, and dies.

Let action be suspended, let characters speak out of character. Let twenty words tell the tale of one. Often none of it affects our enjoyment: the progress of " plot," the illusion of moving reality, is for a space intermitted whilst we surrender to the enchantment of words and a picture or a mood or a quintessential essay on human life. On occasion the plays would be notably duller without the long static speeches. *Richard II* mainly lives on Richard's long speeches. The main action is of no account. There is no surprise or suspense in it, very little interesting movement. It is not merely that it is a chronicle play and we know what had to happen beforehand: so is *Richard III*, but the resource and bravery and brutal candour of that wolf battling against the world keeps us excited until the very end. The second Richard lands, at the beginning of the Third Act, on the coast of Wales with his end predetermined, and a hopeless cadence in his very speeches of firm resolution: the rest of the play is but the prolonged conclusion of what the melodious sensualist, luxuriating in the melancholy of his fall, describes as:

> the tale of lamentable me.

There are moments in the play: Richard's sybarites make a brave brief show before they are led out to death, we are for a time strongly affected by Aumerle, or rather his mother; Richard's smashing of the mirror, and his last sudden fight against surrender (though unhistorical) warms the blood. But the moments are few; the subsidiary characters are not well drawn, hardly drawn at all; and on the whole the interest of the play resides in the long, dramatically diluted speeches, valued for their own sakes. There is Gaunt's " All places that the eye of Heaven visits," there is Bolingbroke's (yes, even Bolingbroke bursts into poetic fantasy), " O who can hold a fire in his hand "; there is Gaunt's glorious speech to York on England, most of which might just as well be a soliloquy—or a platform address. The rest of the play is essentially an elegiac poem. It is Richard, spinning webs of sad fantasy from his mood, brooding over death and the past, toying with thoughts of the future when his own sad end shall be a legend of the chimney-corner, and always in phrases plaintive and liquid as Philomela's or the sad winds sighing:

> Or that I could forget what I have been,
> Or not remember what I must be now,

or vainly offering:

>   my large kingdom for a little grave,
> A little, little grave, an obscure grave,

or conjuring his queen " in winter's tedious nights " to sit by the fire with " good old folks " and exchange her story of a dead king and a grief gone over for their " tales of woeful ages, long ago betide "; or watching his brain and soul begetting " a generation of still breeding thoughts "; for transient intervals only breaking the even level of his mournful melody as with his indignant exclamation against his horse Barbary that carried the usurper, followed instantly by the sorrowful self-reproaching whisper: " Forgiveness, horse." Richard in that mood and with that poet's voice may soliloquize as long as he will, and wander where he will: he obstructs nothing of account; it is Richard that we would hear.

So can Shakespeare enchant us, sometimes when he is most daringly 'holding up' his plot. He ascends with his Muse of Fire, Apollo's finger touches his lips. The matchless verse flows out from him, or such a copious, sparkling babble of prose as Don John, for a scene, speaks, and that was later to ripple divinely, like a merry chime of bells, from Congreve's young queen of coquettes. That facile fluency which, exhibited at table, was subject of complaint by Ben Jonson and, on occasion, extinguished by his mutton-fist thumping the board, would run away with Shakespeare writing; or he would even, did a happy expansion of fancy come to him when he was revising a play, enlarge a speech, already, for the theatre, in peril of the charge of hypertrophy. That he usually succeeds with his digressions is one measure of his magnitude; but it has been a terrible snare to his unwary successors.

The greatest of metrists, the sweetest of singers, the wisest of men, could not be expected to confine himself to the strict requirements of the theatre: he had unique powers and could safely take unique risks, though he usually had a perfect awareness of the limits of safety. But how much harm his example has done to later workers at the ' poetic drama ' it would be impossible to estimate.

Shakespeare's influence is visible almost everywhere in the works of poets who have written plays. A thousand sound lessons in dramatic technique might be derived from him: yet our ' dramatic poets ' usually seem to have no eyes for anything in his works except those things which they had much better not imitate. They copy his distribution of characters, instead of allowing their persons to be generated by the necessities of their plots acting upon their own minds and imaginations; they imitate his language, getting thereby an archaistic and ' bookish ' flavour, which was completely foreign to Shakespeare. Above all, they seem to be much more preoccupied with phrases than with structure, with set speeches than with proper dialogue, sticking purple passages on their scenes as bill-posters stick placards on a wall.

Scarcely one of them (with the notable exception of Browning in *Strafford*) gives the impression that he has ever had the strength to cut out 'good' lines because they would be ineffective or superfluous in the theatre. Continually one meets purple passages whose presence can only be explained on one of two grounds: either the poet has not had the heart to cut them out, or else his sense of the theatre has been so defective, or so under-developed, that he has not even realized that they were out of place. Great and small, they have almost all contributed to that monstrous literary growth, the closet drama: and largely because they have been much more concerned with rivalling Shakespeare than with mastering their themes, much more concentrated on writing resounding or exquisite lines for declamation than with learning even the elements of the dramatic art; the tacit assumption apparently being that any play by a competent poet must be, by right of birth, superior to anything written for the theatre in prose: as though fine words, lofty orations, delicate images, even good characterization and effective backgrounds were in themselves sufficient for the composition of a dramatic masterpiece. The occasional example of Shakespeare has sufficed to justify any dodging of difficulties, any amateurish loading of dialogue with informative description, any amount of poetic padding, any magniloquent irrelevance. Sometimes the attempt to vie with Shakespeare is palpable and direct. Lord Tennyson, though he came to the drama too

DIALOGUE : SOLILOQUIES AND LONG SPEECHES 223

late and flourished in a bad time theatrically, had a considerable dramatist in him. But the vigilant reader of *Queen Mary*, and even *Becket*, cannot help the uneasy feeling that the correct ingredients for a play according to Shakespeare are being kneaded together, citizens, songs and all. Take such a speech as Pole makes to the Queen when she merely asks him whether he has had a good voyage up the river:

> We had your royal barge, and that same chair,
> Or rather throne of purple, on the deck.
> Our silver cross sparkled before the prow,
> The ripples twinkled at their diamond-dance,
> The boats that follow'd were as glowing gay
> As regal gardens; and your flocks of swans,
> As fair and white as angels; and your shores
> Were in mine eyes the queen of Paradise,
> My foreign friends, who dream'd us blanketed
> In ever-closing fog, were much amazed
> To find as fair a sun as might have flash'd
> Upon their lake of Garda, fire the Thames;
> Our voyage by sea was all but miracle;
> And here the river flowing from the sea,
> Not towards it (for they thought not of our
>   tides),
> Seemed as a happy miracle to make glide—
> In quiet—home your banished countryman.

This passage, in spite of some good lines and some accurate observations, is faulty even as verse, particularly as verse for speaking. " Chair, or rather throne," is woolly in this place; the assonance of "tides" and "glide" is ugly; "glowing gay" is stiff; and one really pities the jaws of any actor who should endeavour to speak the line about the "diamond-dance" at once naturally and clearly. Why is it all there? It is difficult to suppose that Tennyson was not remembering, and trying to compete against those other immortal lines about a "barge" that was like a "throne," and had "purple" sails, and "silver" oars. But Shakespeare's description is exquisitely relevant: naturally introduced in reply to a natural question by Agrippa, and necessary to suggest the way in which his "serpent of Old Nile" struck a world's imagination, and his Shakespeare, no doubt, would have made so enchanting a passage desirable even had it been less dramatically essential: we should have loved it and borne with its arrest of things, even had he stuck it in as a parenthesis in *The Merchant of Venice* or *King Lear* away from all the context of Cleopatra. But no man since Shakespeare has been a Shakespeare; and, if the poets continue to write for the stage, the critics of poetry would do well to learn something about the stage and ruthlessly assault those static periods to which we have become so accustomed that we almost take it for granted that a play in verse will consist largely of long speeches in which the characters, whilst action remains suspended, babble of flowers, describe whole histories of past events, launch out into strings of sentimental reminiscences with, "I do remember," or into ardent descriptions of nature such as:

> I rode the hills to-day.
> At dawn, I drank the freedom of the wind
> And heard great waters . . .

which—I hasten to add—is not taken from any particular work.

And if none other can wear Shakespeare's boots, he was sometimes clogged by them himself. There *are* certain speeches in Shakespeare which he does not succeed (to repeat the idiom) in 'getting away with.' There are in many of the plays—*The Merchant of Venice* is a signal example—passages of really good poetry that irritate by their suspension of movement. The Duke's speech in *Measure for Measure*, III. 1, festoons something too freely for the stage, crowded though it is with such phrases as:

> Thy best of rest is sleep,
> And that thou oft provok'st; yet grossly fear'st
> Thy death, which is no more

and:

> Thou hast nor youth nor age;
> But, as it were, an after-dinner's sleep,
> Dreaming on both.

But perhaps the worst example of undramatic verbosity in the whole of Shakespeare is Canterbury's vast speech about the " Salique Law," the French succession, Pepin, Pharamond, Childeric and the rest of it. The Muse of Fire, so lately appealed for, was certainly not ascending " the highest heaven of invention " here. It is a large and diffuse metricization of the chronicles; and were Shakespeare deemed impeccable, would justify a modern poet, eager to get his exposition across at a swoop, in turning into blank verse any article in a Gazetteer or the *Encyclopædia Britannica*. It will, however, be found by the student of Shakespeare's plays in their presumed chronological order (ignoring the doubtful ones) that his mastery over his art, in this as in other regards, steadily increased as time went on.

INDEX

A

Action, unity of, 42
Actors, men in women's parts, 10, 196; importance given to modern, 12; in collaboration with playwrights, 162
Alcibiades, 82–3
All's Well that Ends Well, faulty plot of, 75–6; question of collaboration in, 76; revelation of character in, 160; indication of action in, 190; topical allusion in, 197; use of gibberish in, 201–2
Antony, 70
Antony and Cleopatra, 69–71; Burrows' sonnet on, 13; anachronism in, 31; opening of, 98; telling sentence in, 102; use of unexpected in, 113; typical word of, 116; ending of, 128–9, 194; revelation of character in, 156; use of contrast in, 188; description of barge in, 224
Archer, William, *Play-Making* of, 45
Arthur, Prince, 46–58, 67, 187; revelation of character of, 158
Asides, use of, 205
As You Like It, defect in plot of, 29, 77; sub-plot in, 79–80; Jaques in, 160; dialogue in, 178; long speeches in, 212–14
Audience, 33, 45; Elizabethan, 7, 10, 34, 40; and faulty technique, 39; Shakespeare's references to, 112–13, 196

B

Baker, Professor George P., *Dramatic Technique* of, 16, 45; on choice of words, 168
Barnardine, description of, 106–7

Beatrice, 109–10, 151–2; vocabulary of, 177; repartee of, 183
Benedict, 109–10, 151–2, 183
Bertram, 160
Boccaccio, as source of Shakespeare's plots, 75
Bombast, attack on, 199–200
Boy-actors, in women's parts, 10; and Cleopatra, 196
Bradbrook, Miss, 20; *Elizabethan Stage Conditions* of, 73
Brandes, Dr. George, Shakespearean criticism of, 30–1
Brutus, 69, 100, 121; revelation of character of, 169; oration of, 179
Burrows, Francis, 13

C

Cassius, 107, 180
Catch-phrases, 203
Celia, 29
Chapman, George, 15 *n.*
Charley's Aunt, 35
Chaucer, Geoffrey, as source of plots, 72
Cinthio, *Othello* of, 73
Claudio, 75
Cleopatra, 70; death of, 128–9, 194; off-stage description of, 156
Clowns, Shakespeare's use of, 60
Coleridge, Samuel Taylor, Shakespearean criticisms of, 13, 26–7, 146
Comedies, Shakespeare the creator of English, 59; endings of Shakespeare's, 122–3, 126
Comedy of Errors, The, 101; similarity to *Twelfth Night* in, 119
Conrad, Joseph, descriptions in, 143
Cordelia, husband of, 29, 77; death of, 131–2

227

INDEX

Coriolanus, 68–9; clumsy mechanism of, 84; telling opening in, 102; effective exit in, 111; severity of, 117; conclusion of, 134; description of character in, 150; crowd scene in, 171; indication of action in, 190
Cressida, 70, 72
Cymbeline, opening scene of, 27, 37, 88; anachronisms in, 31; flaws in, 85; reference to time in, 115–16; masque passages in, 117; melodrama in, 118; production of atmosphere in, 188–9; play on words in, 204; asides in, 205

D

Dark Lady of the Sonnets, The, 6–7
Death, 124–6; Shakespeare's awareness of, 123, 126–8
De Quincey, Thomas, Shakespearean criticism of, 23
Dialogue, 43; De Quincey on Shakespeare's, 25; as revealing character, 161 et seq.; functions of, 161; necessary condition of, 162; impossibility of realism in, 163–6; natural sequence in, 182; minor devices in, 195 et seq.; topical allusions in, 195–9; gibberish in, 200–2; malapropism in, 202–3; vituperation in, 203; puns and slapstick in, 204–5; soliloquies and long speeches in, 206 et seq.
Dogberry, 156–7; burlesque of, 199; malapropisms of, 202–3
Drama, poetry in Elizabethan, 5, 7; Greek, 8, 61; modern, 8–12; and modern poets, 11; technique of, see Technique, dramatic; time-condition of, 34, 45; plot of, 42–5; and the novel, 43–5; historical, 61–72; portrayal of character in, 138 et seq.; influence of Shakespeare on, 221–4
Dramatist, minor Elizabethan, 7; difficulties of, 44–5; use of old plots by, 61; description of character by, 138–40, 144; advantages of, over novelist, 140, 144; influence of Shakespeare on, 221–4
Dryden, John, 11
Duncan, 64
Dynasts, The (Hardy), dramatic version of, 11–12, 62

E

Elizabethan drama, poetry of, 5, 7; source of plots of, 61; masques in, 117–18
Elizabethan Stage Conditions (Bradbrook), 73
Elizabethan theatre, scant scenery of, 1, 186, 191–2; stage effects of, 3; minor dramatists of, 7; audiences of, 7, 10, 34, 40; boy-actors of, 10
Euphuism, attack on, 199–200

F

Faerie Queene, Chinese scene in, 2
Faithful Shepherdess, The (Fletcher), 208
Falstaff, Sir John, 29, 68, 79, 192–3; characterization of, 166–7, 170, 175; Chief Justice's reproof to, 176; disclaimed by Henry, 189; euphuisms of, 200; repartee of, 204
Farce, convention of, 35
Flecker, James Elroy, Hassan of, 14, 42
Fletcher, John, and Henry VIII, 65; The Faithful Shepherdess of, 208

G

Gibberish, Shakespeare's use of, 200–2
Gielgud, John, 12
Gloucester, Duke of (Henry VI), 65
Gloucester, Duke of (King Lear), 119–20, 133

INDEX

Granville-Barker, Harley, his preface to *King Lear*, 3–5; on Shakespeare as story-teller, 59; on technical improvisations, 60; on *Julius Cæsar*, 97–98; on the Mask, 117–18; on collaboration of playwright and actor, 161–2; on characterization, 169; on weak line, 170; on scenery and *Hamlet*, 186–7

Greek drama, topicalness of, 8; plots of, 61

Greene, Robert, 15 *n.*

H

Hamlet, pageantry of, 30; technical imperfections of, 35, 77–8, 84; as a novel, 43–4; source of, 77–8; play in, 79; opening scene of, 93–6; revelation of character in, 110, 159; reference to audience in, 112; hiding and listening in, 120; natural dialogue in, 185–187; advice to players in, 196; jests in, 197–8; parodies in, 199; soliloquy in, 210; unnatural speech in, 214–16

Hamlet, revelation of character of, 159–60, 166; soliloquies of, 210

Hardy, Thomas, as Elizabethan dramatist, 11–13; *The Dynasts* of, 11–12, 62 ; scenic descriptions of, 141–3

Hassan (Flecker), 14; a mixture of comedy and tragedy, 42

Hazlitt, William, Shakespearean criticism of, 18, 21

Helena (*All's Well that Ends Well*), 76, 160

Henry IV, 67–8; Falstaff in, 68, 79; flaw in, 85–6; openings of, 101; masterly stage-craft in, 119; indication of action in, 191; indication of scene in, 192

Henry V, 67; prologue to fifth act of, 63; opening of, 99; reference to audience in, 112; scene before Agincourt in, 119; joke against English in, 197; topical allusion in, 198; catchphrase in, 203; soliloquy in, 210; Canterbury's long speech in, 225–6

Henry V, King, 67; soliloquy of, 210

Henry VI, mainly not Shakespeare's, 64–5, 157; defects of, 65, 68; revelation of character in, 157–8, 160

Henry VI, King, 65, 67

Henry VIII, 26; authorship of, 15 *n.*, 64–5, 81; structural weaknesses of, 29, 65–6; begun in Elizabeth's reign, 65 *n.*; descriptions of characters in, 107; references to time in, 115; masque in, 117; argument in, 184

Henry VIII, King, 111

Hermione, 85

Hero, 75

Hewlett, Maurice, 123

Historical dramas, difficulties of, 61–4; those mainly by other hands, 64–6; those mainly by Shakespeare, 66–8

Hubert, 46–58

I

Iago, 28, 74; self-revelation of character of, 158–9; soliloquies of, 210–12

Ibsen, Hendrik, as Elizabethan dramatist, 6

Imogen, 29

J

Jaques, 160, 213–14

John, King, 188

Johnson, Dr., Shakespearean criticism of, 22–3, 59

Jonson, Ben, 220

Juliet, 2, 181

Julius Cæsar, 69; Dr. Brandes on, 31; awkwardness in construction of, 84–5; triumph of stagecraft, 97–8, 108; graphic lines in, 102–3, 108; description of characters in, 107, 155; refer-

INDEX

Julius Cæsar (contd.)
ence to audience in, 112–13; use of unexpected in, 113; references to passage of time in, 115–16; sleep-talking stratagem in, 120–1; pregnant nights in, 121 *n*.; ending of, 135; Mark Antony's oration in, 165–6; crowd-scene in, 171; Cassius' speech in, 180; opening of, 181–2; quarrel in, 184; indication of action in, 191, 193

K

King John, structural weaknesses of, 29, 67; unsuitability of, to modern stage, 40; Hubert and Arthur scene of, 46–58; opening of, 100; description of populace in, 103–4; dialogue in, 172, 187–8; topical allusion in, 197

King Lear, Granville-Barker's preface to, 3–5; Lamb on unactableness of, 3, 19; Swinburne on, 29; short scene in, 40; faults in plot of, 77; subplot in, 79; opening of, 98–9; stratagem of Edgar and Gloucester in, 119–20; end of, 129–134; revelation of character in, 157; Granville-Barker on line in, 170; use of contrast in, 179; use of repetition in, 179–180; pun in, 205; soliloquies in, 208

"Knocking at the Gate in *Macbeth*, The" (De Quincey), 23–5

Kyd, Thomas, 15 *n*.

L

Lamb, Charles, Shakespearean criticism of, 3–4, 18–20
Lear, King, entry of, 99; madness of, 130–1, 179; death of, 132; difficulty in acting, 133; soliloquies of, 208
Lee, Sir Sydney, *Life of Shakespeare* of, 17
Leontes, 189

Life of Shakespeare (Lee), 17
Love's Labour's Lost, indication of character in, 152, 169

M

Macbeth, Tree's presentation of, 2; Lamb on unactableness of, 19; De Quincey on, 24–5; Coleridge on, 27; historical basis of, 64; flaws in, 84; opening scene of, 93, 99; suspense in, 113; reference to time in, 116; porter in, 118; ending of, 135; revelation of character in, 155–6; indication of action in, 193
Macbeth, 155–6
Macbeth, Lady, 64, 84, 155–6
Malapropisms, 202–3
Malvolio, tricking of, 120; soliloquies of, 208
Mamillius, 189
Mark Antony, 165–6
Marlowe, Christopher, 15 *n*.
Marston, John, as Shakespeare's collaborator, 76
Masque, 2, 117–18
Matthews, Professor Brander, 16; on *Othello*, 114
Maugham, Somerset, 12
Measure for Measure, 26; inartistic ending of, 29, 75; question of authorship of, 76; description of character in, 106–7; use of unexpected in, 113; Duke's first speech in, 163; ward-constable in, 196; malapropisms in, 202; unsuccessful speech in, 225
Menenius, 150
Merchant of Venice, The, faults in plot of, 26, 74–5; anatopism in, 31; opening of, 100; off-stage indication of character in, 108, 110, 152–3; long speeches and soliloquies in, 209; suspension of movement in, 225
Mercutio, characterization of, 166; unnecessary speech of, 212

INDEX

Merry Wives of Windsor, The, 103–4; characterization in, 166–7, 170; dialogue in, 175–176; catch-phrase in, 203

Midsummer-Night's Dream, A, Tree's nightingale-machine in, 2; Hazlitt on stage presentation of, 21; play in, 79; Arcadian opulence of, 117; revelation of character in, 152

Miranda, 91–3

Modern drama, 8–12; failings of, 81; and soliloquy, 140, 206–7; rigidity of, 216

Modern theatre, its dependence on scenery and stage effects, 1–3, 12, 40, 191; departure of poetry from, 8, 11–12; mastery of technique in, 22

Moulton, R. G., 16

Much Ado About Nothing, faulty plot of, 75; opening scene of, 88; revelation of character in, 109–10, 151–2, 156–7, 177–8; dialogue in, 177–8, 183; malapropisms in, 202–3

N

Novel, contrasted with drama, 43–5, 138–44

Nym, Corporal, gag of, 203

O

Oliver, 29, 77

Ophelia, 214–15

Orlando, long speech of, 212–13

Othello, 72–4; original story of, 73–4; forcing of plot in, 76–7; openings of, 98, 101; background of, 114; hiding and listening scene in, 120; ending of, 135; revelation of character in, 158–9, 167; use of words in, 168, 190; long speeches in, 208–12

Othello, of Cinthio, 74; declamations of, 208–9

P

Parody, use of, 199–200

Parolles, 190, 201–2

'Pathetic fallacy,' 114, 141

Peele, George, 15 *n.*

Perdita, 148–50; lovely speech of, 217

Pericles, 199; authorship of, 15 *n.*; Swinburne on, 29

Pinero, Sir Arthur, as Elizabethan dramatist, 11

Pistol, bombast of, 200

Play-Making (Archer), 45

Plot, conversion of story into, 42–5

Poetry, in Elizabethan drama, 5, 7–8, 216

Poets, and modern drama, 11–12

Pope, Alexander, on Shakespeare's characters, 144–7, 166

Portia (*Merchant of Venice*), 74–5; lovers of, 106, 108, 152–3

Portia (*Julius Cæsar*), 166

Problem-plays, 8–9

Prologue, Shakespeare's use of, 62–3, 99, 101

Prospero, 91–2

Puns, 204–5

Q

Queen Mary (Tennyson), 223

Quiller-Couch, Sir Arthur, 72

R

Regan, 157, 171

Rescue, The (Conrad), 143

Return of the Native, The (Hardy), 141

Richard II, 67; weakness of subordinate characters in, 29, 219; description of Cotswolds in, 104–5; long speeches in, 218–20

Richard II, King, 66; melancholy speech of, 171, 218–20

Richard III, 65, 67; graphic phrasing in, 105, 189, 191; effective exit in, 111–12; melodrama in, 118; night before Bosworth in, 122; end of, 129; revelation of character in, 154, 172; antiphony in, 181; long speeches in, 218

INDEX

Richard III, King, 66–7
Robertson, J. M., *The Shakespeare Canon* of, 15 *n.*
Romeo, description of, 106; last speech of, 212
Romeo and Juliet, passages in, not written by Shakespeare, 15 *n.*; opening scene of, 27, 89; ending of, 134–5; Nurse in, 158, 173; production of atmosphere in, 189; pun in, 205; long speeches in, 212
Rosalind, 178
Rowe, Nicholas, on Shakespeare's ignoring of rules, 215 *n.*

S

Scenery, modern dependence on, 1–2, 12, 63, 141; description of, in novels, 141–3; and *Hamlet*, 186; Shakespeare's little need for, 191–2
Shakespeare Canon, The (Robertson), 15 *n.*
Shakespeare, William, stagecraft of, 4–5, 112, 116–22; as depicted by Shaw, 6–7; treats of wide issues, 10; exaggeration of grandeur in, 13; collaborators of, 15 *n.*, 17–18, 64–5, 76, 101; books on, 16–17; 'literary' critics of, 18–31; his defiance of unities, 23; long speeches of, 23, 206 *et seq.*; dialogue of, 25, 161 *et seq.*, 195 *et seq.*; opening scenes of, 27, 86–103, 105; his great use of small things, 27, 119; later dramatic style of, 30, 41; anachronisms and anatropisms of, 31–2; technical difficulties of, 35–6, 60; imperfections of, 59–60, 83–6; as story-teller, 59, 105; development of, 59–60, 86, 226; source of plots of, 60–1, 64, 72–8; historical plays of, 62–72; hampered by plots, 72–7; 'underplots' of, 78–81; writes parts for special actors, 80, 140; his skill in construction, 81–2; packed sentences of 102–5, 181; narrative gift of 104; portrayal of character by, 106, 144 *et seq.*, 166–7, 169; use of off-stage description of characters, 106–10, 147, 151–156; movement of characters by, 111; use of suspense by, 113; use of surprise by, 113; backgrounds of, 113–14; knows effect of clocks, 114–16; use of melodrama by, 118; use of contrast by, 118, 178–9, 187; pregnant nights in, 121–122; endings of, 122–3, 126–37; his awareness of death, 123, 126–8; epitaphs of, 127; rare use of irony by, 134; use of soliloquy by, 139–40, 206–12; lucidity of, 162; individualization of speech in, 168–78; ear of, 177; use of iteration by, 179–80; compactness of phrase in, 181–2; repartee in, 183, 204; quarrels in, 184; indication of action in, 190–4; indication of scene in, 192; topical allusions in, 195–9; parodies of style in, 199–200; use of gibberish, 200–2; malapropisms in, 202–3; catchphrases in, 203; use of vituperation, 203; puns in, 204–5; slap-stick in, 205; unnecessary speeches in, 212–16; lovely passages in, 216–18, 220; songs in, 217; dangers of imitating, 221–6; unsuccessful speeches in, 225–6
Shaw, George Bernard, as Elizabethan dramatist, 6; Shakespeare of, 6–7
Shylock, revelation of character of, 110–11, 153; long speech and soliloquy of, 209
Sly, Christopher, 77, 101
Soliloquy, 139–140, 206–12
Spectacle, influence of, 2
Stage-effects, 2–3
Swinburne, Algernon Charles, *Study of Shakespeare* of, 28–30

INDEX 233

T

Taming of the Shrew, The, 77; opening scene in, 88; comic lesson in, 119; slapstick in, 205

Technique, dramatic, 21, 33-7; examples of bad, 37-9; and the audience, 39; changes in, 39-40; general principles of, 41; books on, 45

Tempest, The, 81; opening of, 90-3, 182; masque passages of, 117; dialogue in, 174

Tennyson, Lord, imitation of Shakespeare by, 222-4

Tess of the D'Urbervilles, 141-3

Theatre, Shakespeare's references to, 195-7. *See* Elizabethan Theatre; Modern Theatre

Thersites, 120, 203

Timon of Athens, weaknesses in, 82-3; description of character in, 154

Titus Andronicus, 68; authorship of, 15 n., 68; anachronism of, 31-2

Tragedies, endings of, 122-3, 127-37; beginnings of, 126

Tree, Sir Herbert, stage effects of, 2

Troilus, 70, 99-100

Troilus and Cressida, 69-72; Swinburne on, 30; anachronisms in, 31; question of collaboration in, 76; opening of, 99-100; suggestion of atmosphere in, 103, 114; hiding and listening scene in, 120; ironic ending to, 134; revelation of character in, 154, 158; dialogue in, 172-3; compactness of utterance in, 181; debate in, 183

Twelfth Night, opening of, 100; off-stage indication of character in, 108-9; favourite stage devices in, 119-20; dialogue in, 174-5; use of gibberish in, 201

Two Gentlemen of Verona, anatopism in, 31; similarity to *Twelfth Night* in, 119

U

Unities, Shakespeare's defiance of, 23

W

Winter's Tale, The, anachronisms of, 32; flaws in, 85; indication of character in, 147-50, 153-4, 172, 189; poetic speech in, 217

Wolsey, Cardinal, 107